Liking Myself Back

Liking Myself Back

AN INFLUENCER'S JOURNEY
FROM SELF-DOUBT
TO SELF-ACCEPTANCE

JACEY DUPRIE

WITH JODI LIPPER

PARK
ROW
BOOKS

PARK
ROW
BOOKS™

ISBN-13: 978-0-7783-1190-4

Liking Myself Back: An Influencer's Journey from Self-Doubt to Self-Acceptance

Park Row Books
22 Adelaide St. West, 41st Floor
Toronto, Ontario M5H 4E3, Canada
ParkRowBooks.com
BookClubbish.com

Printed in U.S.A.

To my parents for letting me share my early chapters.
And to Grant for the ones we've yet to write.

Liking Myself Back

Introduction

BEFORE STARTING MY BLOG, *DAMSEL IN DIOR*, BEFORE
traveling around the world to fashion shows and working
with designers, and even before Instagram existed, I was a
farmer's daughter from South Texas. The cotton harvest season fell in the middle of summer, and there was a constant
film of humidity that stuck to the wind and blew through
the fields. I rarely wore shoes, and my messy, sweaty hair
was held back in a baseball cap. On my family's fifteen-
hundred-acre farm, there wasn't much to do. I spent my
days circling the farm on my four-wheeler, raising hogs for
the 4-H club, or digging mud castles in my backyard without a friend or neighbor in sight.

Most often, I escaped into the vivid world of my imagination. I especially loved playing dress-up. With the right costume, I could sing at the Grand Ole Opry, I could fight pirates at sea, I could tumble down a rabbit hole as Alice in Wonderland, or I could be a princess finding her happily-ever-after. For a while, it was fun and carefree and innocent, a way to pass the time and stretch my mind to imagine life's possibilities beyond the endless white sea of cotton that surrounded me.

As I got older, my life grew more complicated, and so did my relationship with clothes. Alcohol was a big part of the culture I grew up in. As a child, I rarely saw an adult who wasn't holding a drink, and every pickup truck seemed to contain an ice chest filled with beer. The words *alcoholic* or *addict* didn't punctuate the vocabulary of the people in my hometown, but drinking was a big part of most farmers' identities. While most of them drank socially without it negatively affecting their lives or livelihoods, alcohol slowly but surely took complete control over my dad. By the time I was in my teens, he was a full-blown addict, my parents' marriage was crumbling, and my idyllic childhood had spiraled into chaos.

At that point, my life at home became something I truly needed to escape from—not just for fun, but in order to survive. And I found myself playing dress-up once again, but this time with carefully curated items that presented an image of perfection to the outside world. I fell in love with fashion, glamorous, high-end, brand-name fashion, because it gave me a chance to be someone besides the lost little damsel in distress I often felt myself to be.

People always say to dress for the life you want, and I believed that if I was wearing the right clothes, I could transform myself from someone who was deeply scarred by my childhood into a confident, self-assured young woman with a beautiful, happy life. When it felt like everything was completely out of my hands, I controlled the narrative the only way I knew how—by presenting a false image of perfection to hide how I truly felt. My clothes, hair, and style were on point, while inside I was, quite honestly, a mess.

Ironically (or not!), this basically became my job. As a blogger and influencer, my job is to share my life with my followers on my blog and on social media and to make things look pretty and perfect, regardless of what is really going on behind the scenes. I had unknowingly been preparing to be an influencer my entire life, long before such a job ever existed. But, funny enough, dressing as a confident, empowered, professional woman and sharing these images with the world didn't heal my wounds or change how I felt about myself inside. And no number of likes or follows or shares made me feel any closer to the person I was pretending to be.

In fact, living through such a public lens and putting so much focus on how I looked and what I wore took an enormous toll on my mental health. For years, I suffered from crippling self-doubt and depression as I lived my adult life as if I were still a traumatized kid trying to escape from home. I had everything I'd ever thought I wanted: front-row seats at fashion week shows, free stays in luxurious hotel suites around the globe, and a closetful of high-end labels. But none of it mattered. Until I looked at what was hiding underneath all those beautiful clothes and filtered pictures, I could never be truly happy.

It took almost losing my marriage for me to wake up and start peeling back the layers to find out who I really was and what I really wanted. I did the work—the unglamorous, daily slog—of healing from my childhood. I set healthy boundaries between my life and my work to protect my mental health. And along the way, I slowly found my way back to that innocent love of fashion I'd had as a young girl, who saw the world with a sense of wonder and infinite possibility.

Instead of hiding the truth of who I am or creating a false image, my clothes now show off the real me. No, I'm not perfect, but I'm done trying to be. Instead of finding my worth in labels and metrics, I've reclaimed what is authentic and meaningful, away from the glossy sheen of my online life. After years of self-doubt, self-criticism, and even, at times, self-hatred, I'm finally liking myself back.

1

Filtered

I SWITCHED MY PHONE OUT OF AIRPLANE MODE JUST moments after we touched down at JFK and scanned the influx of texts, looking for a message from my husband, Grant. When I'd left that morning, we'd been arguing about him coming with me. Or, more accurately, him *not* coming with me. We were four years into our marriage, and I'd mostly given up on asking him to join me when I traveled for work, which was pretty much constantly. But this time, I really wanted him there, to be with me as a part of this world I'd created for myself.

This trip would keep me away from our home in LA for a total of twelve days, including my time in New York for meetings and my final stop in Paris for fashion week.

I was speaking on a ShopStyle panel in Paris and hoping for a last-minute invitation to my very first Dior show. But instead of feeling excited, I was just empty. For so long, Grant had been my life partner and my best friend, but now he was slowly slipping further and further away from me.

"You'll be too busy to miss me," Grant had told me. "And besides, no one needs Mr. Damsel hanging around." He was poking fun at the name of my blog, *Damsel in Dior*, the name he'd come up with four years before. I knew how much he hated it when people called him that, and I didn't blame him one bit. But it also didn't feel fair for him to respond by pulling away from me and the blog that had gone from a hobby to a job to basically taking over my entire life.

Finally, I came to his text. Hope you landed okay, it said, with a kiss emoji.

Landed safe, I replied with my own kiss, and then switched on the "Let's Walk in New York" playlist that I made specifically for my trips to the city. "Sinnerman" by Nina Simone blasted through my headphones as I craned my neck to look out the plane window and up at the sky. It was already nighttime in New York, and the sky was dark. No matter how many times I visited, I never got used to the fact that in the city there were never any stars.

Where I grew up in South Texas, the sky was a glittering tapestry. At night, the farm was pitch-dark, and the only lights we could see in the distance were from the nearest town about seven miles away. My mom, dad, older brother, Justin, and I would lie on our backs on a big trampoline in the yard. As the surface beneath us rocked gently, my dad would point out the different stars in the Milky Way galaxy. Then he'd go on to tell us about the northern lights. It only happened during certain months of the year and in certain places, he told us, but it was a special magic show that danced across the sky. He promised us that one day we would see it.

When it came to constellations, meteorology, outer space, and tall tales, my dad was an expert. More important, he stressed the value of wishing on stars as he taught us, "Star light, star bright, first star I see tonight, I wish I may, I wish I might, have the wish I wish tonight." Always with the warning, "Be careful what you wish for," my dad instilled in me the faith that whatever you wished for and believed in enough could, in fact, come true.

An hour after landing, I was exhausted as I walked through the lobby of the Four Seasons Hotel. I loved dressing up for my trips to New York because it gave me an opportunity to wear all black and pull my matching black Louis Vuitton carry-on luggage, which was the biggest purchase I'd ever made for myself, with my black Saint Laurent tote resting on top. It felt super "corporate," and I hoped that when people looked at me they saw a boss.

"Welcome back, Ms. Duprie," the woman at the front desk said as soon as she saw me. "Your room is ready for you. Here's your key." The staff was always so kind that they made New York feel almost like a second home. So, even though I was exhausted and my whole body craved the bed, I couldn't go before asking a few questions about her family and her ten-year-old son.

It was a relief to slide open the door to my room a few

minutes later, flop off my black Gianvito Rossi pumps, and collapse onto the bed. The hotel bedding was white and cool against my cheek. The television had the Four Seasons welcoming screen on display, filling the room with classical music and showcasing all their properties around the world. For a moment, I thought about which locations I wanted to visit, but the idea of traveling to all those beautiful places solo was too depressing. I forced myself to push those thoughts aside as I turned my head and glanced into the pristine wood-and-gray marble bathroom. I couldn't wait to hop into the deep soaking tub.

Out of the corner of my eye, I saw a beautiful bouquet of pink peonies (my favorite) sitting on the small corner table. I smiled as tears pricked my eyes, and I felt something like hope. Grant had been thinking of me. Maybe things weren't as bad as I'd feared. I got up and opened the card. "Welcome back," it read, and was signed from the Four Seasons' housekeeping staff. My heart sank, realizing the flowers weren't from Grant at all. On one hand, the fact that the staff knew me well enough to know my favorite flowers and have them sent to my room seemed indicative of a fabulous lifestyle. It was something I had only seen in the movies growing up. But inside, traveling to these fabulous places alone felt pathetic. And on top of that, I felt guilty for not enjoying it more.

My lesser instincts sensed an opportunity, though. I could use the flowers as an excuse to make Grant feel bad for not showing me the same care and attention as the Four Seasons' staff.

I grabbed my phone and called home.

"Hey, babe, how's New Yawk," Grant answered in a fake, over-the-top Brooklyn accent.

"Thank you so much for the flowers!" I said in a fake upbeat voice. "They're so pretty." There was an awkward silence, of course. "Oh, wait," I said as I pretended to find the card and read it, "they're from the housekeeping staff." I winced, listening to myself. I had wanted to make Grant feel bad, or to make him angry, or to get some sort of reaction, anything to shake us out of our boring routine. But I knew deep down that Grant didn't really deserve this.

"I'm sorry," he said, writing it off with a joke. "Of all the people I thought I had to be jealous of..."

"At least someone was thinking of me." There was another pause. "I need to unpack. Let's talk tomorrow."

But instead of unpacking, I sat at the edge of the bed and bit my nails, staring out the window at the dark starless sky.

For a moment, I thought about how far I had come. Growing up, money wasn't something we generally had a lot of, and neither was opportunity. In South Texas, the only women I knew with full-time jobs were teachers, nurses, or stay-at-home moms. It was beyond rare for someone to venture out to LA or New York City, not to mention to create their own lifestyle blog. And look at me. I was married, had a successful business, and got to wear high-end fashions and travel around the world as my actual job. By every external standard, I had made it. But despite all that, I couldn't help but wonder where I had gone wrong.

I had worked so hard to achieve all of the things I believed would make me happy, but I was left feeling disappointed, like some important piece was missing. I didn't feel fulfilled, and not having Grant there to share it with me made all of my achievements feel worthless. I was so far from understanding then that by focusing so much of my time and energy on my work and so little on my marriage or myself, I was the one who had made it all feel cheap. But I was at least aware enough to realize that something was wrong. Had I made the wrong wish or wished too hard on the wrong star?

I moved over to a cushioned bench in front of the window and looked out at the high-rise buildings across the street. When I traveled alone, I often passed the time by spotting a neighboring apartment with the light on. If I was lucky, I could spy into the window and peek into someone else's life. For a brief moment, I let my imagination drift as I wondered what their life was like. What did they do for a living? Where were they coming home from that evening and who were they coming home to? Did they ever look out of the window toward my hotel room and wonder the same things about me?

It was close to midnight when I closed the curtain and tucked myself into bed with my cell phone carefully placed under my pillow. Rather than focus on the loneliness in my heart, I closed my eyes and thought about all of the outfits I wanted to shoot myself wearing the next morning. Eventually, I drifted off to sleep.

I woke up at six thirty the next morning, ready to push aside my thoughts from the night before and don my emotional armor. I was an expert at stuffing down my feelings and distracting myself with work, and it was time to put my worries about my marriage and lack of fulfillment

away and get down to business. It was a relief to know
that I would be too busy over the next couple of days to
even think. When I felt unfulfilled, I took it as a sign that
I needed to be doing more or working harder instead of
stopping to reevaluate what I was doing or realign my pri-
orities. Work was an escape, a much-needed break from
the thoughts and feelings that I didn't know how to face.

The first thing I did that morning was order breakfast from room service before getting dressed in my first
of many outfits for the day. A fruit platter, bread basket,
orange juice and coffee for two, along with eggs, bacon,
and a nice big waffle. This gigantic breakfast was purely
for the art of the flat lay. These photos were very trendy
on Instagram at the time, and consisted of a beautifully
laid out spread of various foods, ranging in colors and tex-
tures. I always added a copy of the *New York Times* within
the frame of my flat-lay photos. By the time I finally captured an image that was worthy of posting, the food was
cold, and I was running late. So, I settled for a quick bite
of bacon and a few swigs of coffee.

I threw on my Zimmermann dress and raced downstairs to meet my photographer, Alexandra, to get some
shots of me on the street and in the hotel lobby before I
headed off for a full day of meetings. The pictures you'd
see on social media from bloggers and influencers at this
time were not just random shots taken in real time over
the course of a day. They were meticulously planned out
and professionally shot and styled like an editorial spread
in a magazine. I also paid for my stay by posting photos
of the hotel on my blog and social media. It was a trade.

I posted photos of my breakfast with the *New York Times*, me walking in and out of the lobby, and taking baths in the beautiful tub, and the hotel usually put me up for free. It was a win-win for everyone.

After three outfit changes and an hour of shooting, I felt that we had what we needed. I climbed into the back of the SUV that would serve as my office for the day and looked at my printed itinerary. I was diagnosed with ADHD when I was in fifth grade, and have spent much of my life finding coping strategies that help me function as well as possible. If I didn't have everything printed out in front of me, I never would have ended up at the right place at the right time or remembered the name of anyone I was meeting with. I also had reminders and alerts popping up constantly on my phone to post sponsored content, remember scheduled calls, remind me of people's birthdays (including my own mom's), and anything else that I couldn't afford to forget.

The columns on my itinerary listed the name of the person I was meeting with, the fashion brand they represented, where and when we were meeting, and perhaps most important, everything I'd learned about them over the course of previous calls, emails, and meetings: birthdays, anniversaries, favorite foods, the names of their kids, their hobbies, and any other interesting tidbits. When I met with PR reps for brands, my goal was to talk about anything other than fashion and find something else we had in common so we could start building real relationships. More than anything, I have these relationships to thank for my success.

After each coffee or lunch, I furiously scribbled down notes in the back of the SUV so I could remember the details the next time we met. This wasn't merely a strategic move to make these people feel special. They actually were important to me, and I didn't want to make them feel unimportant because of my own forgetfulness. At the time, I had very few friends outside of work, as I spent most of my free time with industry people instead of the rest of my friends and family. I wanted my industry friends to know how special they were to me, and not just because of their power or position.

Without these notes, I had zero chance of remembering anything from our meetings. I have forgotten the start dates of new jobs (and lost the jobs as a result), forgotten to take important medications, and have even forgotten my own age. I never wanted others to see me as a "ditzy blonde." I longed to be respected and seen as smart, sharp, and together, not dumb and forgetful. Rather than feel defeated and frustrated by my ADHD diagnosis, I wanted to take control of it. I even made it a fun challenge for myself to see how much intel I could gather about a person to bring up in future meetings. I silently gave myself a gold star when I randomly surprised someone mid-conversation with a fun fact that I remembered from our previous meeting.

Sometimes the connections I made in these meetings led to lucrative partnership deals. Sometimes they led to invitations to exclusive fashion week shows and events. Sometimes just getting a meeting with the brand felt like a huge victory. On this trip, the meeting I was the most excited about was with the in-house PR rep at Chanel. I'd been reaching out to their team for years, asking them to grab coffee and sending them the pictures of me wearing Chanel that I'd posted on the blog and social media. Finally, I was introduced to their beauty team and had slowly worked my way over to the fashion side. Sometimes the door into a high-fashion house wasn't the one I'd originally gone knocking on, but I knew they didn't open their doors very often. So, anytime an entry was cracked, I'd slither my way in and find the room I wanted once I was inside.

After I'd sweet-talked the Chanel beauty team for over a year, they finally introduced me to Natasha, the head of PR for the fashion team at Chanel. I nervously picked at my nails as the SUV pulled down 57th Street toward the Chanel flagship store between 5th Avenue and Madison. Once I was on the street, I steadied my pace just before opening the black glass office doors next door to the store so I didn't seem too eager to get inside. After checking in with the security desk, I was given a badge and told to take the elevator up to the fourteenth floor. "Breathe," I told myself. I tried calming my nerves by counting to four with each inhalation and again with each exhalation, a method I'd learned in yoga.

The elevator doors opened, and there stood Natasha, looking exactly how I'd pictured. She was tall, slim, had on little to no makeup, and wore a perfectly styled label-less outfit. Her sincere smile and French accent immediately welcomed me into her office, and my nerves melted away. We sat down and began to talk about all things career-related, life-related, and I was able to make her laugh when I shared my story about getting lost on the subway on a previous trip to New York. These meetings always felt a bit like first dates, and this one left me feeling confident that there would be a second date. Maybe even a third.

Just before I left, Natasha complimented me on the sweater I was wearing. I had just ordered it from Net-a-Porter, and it was tan with black stripes. It felt amazing to know that she actually thought it was cool.

Just as we were about to hug goodbye, Natasha asked, "Are you planning to be in Paris this season?"

My heart nearly jumped out of my chest. "Yes, I am," I replied steadily.

"Well, hopefully we can find a place for you at the show," she said.

We said goodbye, and I kept telling myself not to get too excited. It was hard to allow myself to believe that the dream of attending the Chanel Fashion Week show could ever come true. But that meeting was a nice reminder that possibilities can live outside of our greatest imagination.

That day, I also met with the PR reps from Shopbop, Intermix, Splendid, and Ralph Lauren before heading to a Veuve Clicquot champagne launch at the Chelsea. It was always funny to me how the PR reps tended to perfectly match the brands they worked for. Elizabeth from Ralph Lauren was brunette, all-American, and preppy. The girls from Shopbop were younger and dressed trendier, with black eyeliner from the night before still smudged underneath their eyes. And, of course, Natasha had been the perfect representative for Chanel.

The next day was just as packed with meetings, and I

added in stops to three showrooms to borrow clothes to wear during my week in Paris. Besides getting that all-important face time with brands, this was the main reason I always stopped in New York on the way to Paris Fashion Week. When I was starting out, I would buy items from the more affordable brands, like J.Crew or Splendid, and create content to show them. Then I would reach out and say how much my followers loved their clothes, that I was already wearing them, and that I would love to post photos of me in Paris wearing their stuff. Eventually, they started inviting me to come in and borrow clothes. Another win–win.

This was common practice in the fashion industry. For years, brands had been sending their clothes out for celebrities to wear to events and in pictures. This was now becoming more common with bloggers. Every time a brand let me borrow clothes, I was so grateful and made sure to treat the items with special care. I always had the clothes dry-cleaned before returning them wrapped in tissue paper, with a handwritten note and maybe a small gift of thanks. I knew that, in general, publicists were overworked and underappreciated. They often complained about celebrities borrowing clothes, wearing them out to clubs, and returning them smelling like cigarette smoke. So, these small gestures that came naturally to me also helped me stand out from the pack.

With my meetings done and my two extra suitcases filled with the clothes I'd pulled from the showrooms, I boarded the plane for Paris. My frequent flights were my escape, and I craved them when I was on the ground. Yet, as soon as the wheels lifted and I was trapped alone in the cabin, I felt suffocated. The thoughts and emotions I had been too busy to entertain while I was in New York began to rise to the surface. In my seat, I could escape from my daily life, but there was no hiding from the wave of emotions that always hit me. I tried to sleep, but the cabin was hot, and I felt restless. Every time I started to nod off, my dry mouth caked my throat closed and my heavy head lifted up for a swig of water.

Instead of sleeping, I looked out the window at the clouds below. They reminded me of the white clouds on the wallpaper my mom had let me pick out for the closet in my childhood room. I loved that wallpaper, and my closet was my safe, secret hiding place whenever my dad drank or my parents fought. (Those two things usually went together.) Too often, my weekends started with me lying on the blue carpet of my closet floor, counting the clouds on my wallpaper as I listened to my mom screaming at my dad about how she wanted him to come with us to church or the fact that it was too early in the morning for him to start drinking vodka.

Once the yelling finally stopped, my mom usually came into my room and asked if I wanted to go shopping. She knew there was no question that I wanted to escape. First, we'd get out a fashion magazine and try to figure out which outfits we thought we could replicate as closely as possible with clothes from JCPenney, Target, and Old Navy. Then we'd take a forty-five-minute drive to the nearest shopping center and see what we could find.

For us, shopping usually meant window-shopping. Money

was extremely scarce and we were always on a tight budget. Those trips to window-shop and try things on were a frequent escape from the chaos of home. Once or twice a year when we actually bought things, the clothes we brought back with us felt like an armor for me to wear at school, one that attempted to hide my messy home life.

Staring out of the tiny airplane window at the clouds, I choked back a bitter laugh. Nothing had changed. The clothes I wore now to mask my true feelings were just a lot nicer.

I didn't know as many people in Paris as I did in New York and had fewer meetings lined up. So, there was more time for me to wander the streets by myself. It was on this part of the trip that I really started to wish Grant would agree to travel with me. Sitting alone in quaint French cafés, I couldn't understand why I wasn't sharing my cappuccino and croissant with my best friend.

I was attending a few shows that fashion week. But the first thing I did when I arrived was reach out to my contact at Dior. "I'm here in Paris," I wrote. "If you have a last-minute opening, I would be honored to attend the show." The first time I'd gone to Paris Fashion Week, just two years before, I wasn't invited to any shows. But I firmly believed that if I wanted to be somewhere, whether it was a neighborhood I dreamed of living in or a fashion show in a fabulous city, the first step was to just show up. Through cold calls and relentless outreach, little by little I started to get to know more people and receive invitations.

My first day in Paris, I attended a collection preview

for Oscar de la Renta on Rue Saint-Honoré, which was simply a chance to see their new collection presented on mannequins instead of models, followed by a full runway show for Lacoste at Jardin des Tuileries. When I got back to the hotel that night, I saw that I had gotten a response from my contact at Dior. "We'd love to have you attend," it read, with a pdf attachment of the invitation.

I stared at the invite for a few seconds too long, not quite believing it was real. Then I let out a squeal and did a little happy dance around my hotel room before quickly shifting into panic mode. The show was the very next day. The small handful of bloggers that had already been invited had been posting pics of the invitation and the bag or clothes that Dior had sent them along with it for days. I was at least five steps behind the eight ball.

Worst of all, I didn't have a single item from the brand to wear to the show. That's right—the "Damsel in Dior" didn't own one piece of Dior. This was ironic, but it was also sort of the point. When I'd first started the blog, I wanted to show my readers that they didn't have to wear high-end designer labels to feel like they were dressed in Dior. No matter what they were wearing, they could model themselves after a woman in Dior, who I imagined never felt ugly, or worthless, or insecure. Instead, I pictured her walking out the door every day with the confidence that she could do anything and be anything and have anything that she wanted.

A Damsel in Dior didn't feel helpless or lost, as I often did as I was growing up and even as a young woman— the classic damsel in distress waiting for someone or something to come and save me. Rather, a Damsel in Dior felt in control of her entire life, no matter what she was wearing. I longed to capture this feeling for myself and for the women who followed my blog.

As I pieced together the best outfit I could come up with that day in Paris, I definitely did not feel completely confident or in control. The day's agenda included speaking at a ShopStyle panel, attending the Balenciaga show, the Dior show, and then ending with an Estée Lauder party that night. What could possibly be appropriate for all of those events? I finally landed on a sleeveless black top from Sandro with sheer polka-dot cutouts along the neck and sides with a white midi-length skirt, Prada heels, and a Balenciaga bag. I was hoping that my look wouldn't scream about the fact that I wasn't dressed in Dior, but instead lend itself to the classic and sophisticated tone of the event. The Damsel in Dior was attending Dior sans Dior—oh, the tragedy.

I was unsure of my outfit, but I headed into the ShopStyle breakfast panel feeling confident about the job I was there to do. I was talking about the business of blogging to a roomful of editors. While I'd never loved public speaking, I knew there was nothing they could throw at me that I wouldn't have an answer for. For four years, I had completely immersed myself in learning everything there was to know about social media, marketing, social engagement, algorithms, and conversion rates. I loved trying to figure out why my followers bought what they did, the analytics behind their behavior. I explained how important it was to post consistently, both in terms of the frequency and type of content they posted.

"Your viewers need to know what to expect from you, especially when you are growing your following," I explained to the editors who filled the room. "For example, you aren't going to find a spread of bikini shots in *Architectural Digest*, are you?" I paused for a few laughs. "The same thing goes for your social media feed. Try to focus on the categories you want to post in, such as beauty and fashion, and share the same types of content consistently. Maybe an outfit photo on Mondays and a new beauty product on Wednesdays. Always try to post on consistent days. So, if you do a fashion post on Mondays and a beauty post on Wednesdays, you can add something fun and quirky on Fridays. But try not to post a random photo that doesn't really match your feed or your brand. It will throw off your audience on what to expect."

I also shared data about the best time of day to post, and what type of content to include in newsletters and blogs versus social media. I had fewer followers on Instagram than many of my fellow influencers, but there was so much value in my blog's loyal readers. Even then, I knew how important it was to own my own domain. My blog was my own real estate on the internet, and I encouraged everyone to have their own stake.

As they filed out, many people stopped me to say how much they'd learned from my talk. It felt great to know that I had nailed it, but the high from that panel quickly wore off. In the car on the way to the Balenciaga show, I checked Instagram to find some horribly hurtful comments left on the last picture I'd posted.

Not my top choice of shoe with that dress. *She's right,* I thought.

Wow, her face is really starting to show her age. *I know,* I thought. *I'm getting Botox as soon as I get back to LA.*

Her poor husband never travels with her. I wonder what's up with that! *Dammit,* I thought. *They can see right through me.*

Are you pregnant?

I rolled my eyes and tried to set it aside, but these comments and more like them raced through my mind throughout the rest of the day. While I was putting every ounce of energy into building my brand and my audience, it became a slippery slope in which I found myself seeking validation and acceptance from the strangers who followed me on the internet. These people apparently knew me better than many of my best friends, who were at home raising families and going to their "real" jobs in corporate America and had little idea of what was really going on with me.

While I was posting about intimate moments of my life—photos of myself in the bathtub, sitting in a taxicab between meetings, or sitting alone on a bar stool, it felt like my followers were right there with me, experiencing everything that I was experiencing. And when I failed to gain their approval, it cut deeply. It felt like an attack.

My emotional state continued to devolve throughout the day. At the Balenciaga show, I was seated behind the other bloggers in attendance, which compounded my feelings of insecurity. I sat there breathing deeply, and lied to myself that where I sat at a show didn't really matter. But it did.

It mattered to me. Fashion show attendees were basically seated in order of importance, and I took my seating assignment as a sign that I wasn't working hard enough. The whole "you can't sit with us" movement in the fashion industry was in full effect. It wasn't so much that I was told I couldn't sit in the front row; I just wasn't invited (yet). And I was so disconnected from my self-worth that my seat assignment at one show could rattle my confidence for days.

I had a quick break for lunch and to take some pictures for the blog. By the time I was stepping carefully down the cobblestone streets toward the Louvre, where the Dior show was being held, I was exhausted from the highs and lows of the day. Yet, as I approached the iconic glass pyramid, I felt a swoop deep in my stomach. I had been waiting for this moment for so long, and now here I was, feeling very much on display. Would everyone notice that I wasn't wearing Dior? Would this clue them in to the fact that I didn't truly belong? Would the trolls call me out for my awful outfit? I felt like a new kid on the first day of school, hoping I'd worn the right thing and that I could somehow, against all odds, find a way to fit in.

I took my seat and looked around me in awe. There was Anna Wintour in the front row, of course, and Bill Cunningham, the famous fashion photographer, racing around quietly while snapping photos of fashion's elite. I had just seen these people at fashion shows in New York, and being in Paris with them now made me feel like on some level I really was one of them. Never mind the fact that I was sitting near the back, that I had only been invited to fill the empty seat after someone else had backed out. I was still here.

A smile crept onto my face as I continued to look around at the gathering crowd. Finally, I saw another familiar face: Tina, a wildly successful blogger who I'd become friendly with over the past few years.

"Hi!" I called out enthusiastically as she walked past my row.

"Oh, hey," she replied with a slight nod as she continued on to her seat. My smile froze on my face as I hid my hands under my bag, not wanting her or anyone else to see the damage I had done to my nails.

I always hated the fact that I bit my nails. It was something I did in secret, when I was alone, but the evidence itself was so visible, and my bitten nails made me feel like an ugly little child instead of a confident grown woman. Whenever I saw a woman with perfectly manicured nails, I assumed that she had her entire life together.

I have never been that person. No matter how hard I try, I always have a few strands of hair out of place, my nails are always bitten down, and my makeup is always a touch smudged. To me, these imperfections symbolize the fact that my life has always felt a bit rough around the edges. Undone. At the time, I desperately tried to hide all evidence of these flaws because I believed that if I wasn't perfect, I was worthless. Accepting them as part of me came much later, and with many years of practice.

Suddenly, the lights went off, and the huge open white space was completely thrown into darkness. I looked around nervously as my eyes slowly adjusted, not knowing what was going on. The lights were dimmed just long enough for me to ask myself, "Wait, is there a power outage?" But everyone around me was calm. After about thirty seconds, music started to play and the lights came back on, and I realized it had been their way of hushing the crowd to start the show.

I couldn't hide the grin on my face as I turned my full attention to the four interconnecting circular runways in front of me. The models walked from circle to circle so that every seat, even mine in the nosebleeds, had a great view. My favorite look was a dress that had an edgy black top with cutouts and a white princess skirt, paired with high black boots. This juxtaposition between edgy and girlie was exactly how I liked to dress, and it was a pleasant surprise to see that the look somewhat mirrored the one I had frantically pieced together that morning.

The music blasted so loudly that it vibrated under my seat, mirroring the feelings that were pounding in my heart. It was as if the models were marching directly to the beat of the music. This wasn't just a fashion show, and it didn't feel like a concert, either. It was a full-bodied sensory experience that combined all the things I loved about my job: fashion, photography, music, creativity, and a damn good show.

I glanced around at the faces watching the show and zeroed in on the dark glasses belonging to Anna Wintour, the chief editor of *Vogue*. I wondered what she was thinking as I studied her trademark smirky grin and followed her head as it moved from side to side when each model passed by. I noticed that she didn't have a handbag with her. She only carried her cell phone, and she didn't snap a single photo the entire time.

This was very much unlike the international fashion bloggers who sat a few sections away from her, also in the front row. These girls all lifted their phones in unison, like they had each received a secret memo about the exact looks they should photograph for their Instagram feeds. I watched them all looking so effortless and cool tapping their feet to the beat of the music and whispering into one another's ears as if they were lifelong besties.

I longed to be seated in the front row so I could have what I believed that seat assignment represented—belonging, acceptance. I pushed down these thoughts and forced my eyes back to the models themselves, focusing on the visceral experience before me. I don't think I took a single breath before it was suddenly over and I was spit back out onto the gray cobblestone street.

My head was still spinning when I got back to my hotel room that night. I felt so excited and inspired, and I couldn't wait to tell someone about it. I quickly phoned Grant, but he was in the middle of a meeting and couldn't talk. He was a real-estate developer, and was working on a new work-live loft unit in Los Angeles that had taken the past three years to develop. There was no one else in my life who might understand why the show had been so exciting to me. Feeling deflated, I slumped onto the bed. But I wasn't ready for the night to be over. I wanted validation for the amazing experience I'd just had.

Instead of getting undressed, I went into the bathroom and freshened up my hair and makeup. Once I deemed myself selfie-ready, I started snapping pictures until I got one that I wanted to post. Satisfied that my photo and caption contained all the enthusiasm needed to show how thrilled and blessed I felt about the day's events, I finally got into my pj's and waited for the likes and comments to start rolling in. Only, no number of likes would have ever been enough to connect the real me with the smiling girl in the photo. Feeling a little silly and sorry for myself, I popped an Ambien, put my phone away, turned out the lights, and tried to sleep.

"Hey!" I clamored into the house wheeling my luggage behind me a few days later.

"Welcome home." Grant quickly looked up from his laptop, and then finished what he was doing before getting up to help me with my bags. "How was your flight?"

Grant and I had a house rule that we would never pick each other up from the airport, especially in traffic-laden Los Angeles. We always saw eye to eye about what a pointless effort it was and had decided long before to give each other the gift of never having to do it. We also never brought home gifts outside of little stuffed animals from the airport that we gave to our two English bulldogs, William and Polly.

"The flight felt so long," I said and gave him a kiss. It was still morning in LA, and although I was tired from the flight, I felt the call of my email and everything else that was waiting to be done. "I'm gonna go check on the office."

After every trip, arriving home was when the real work

began. First, my assistant, Haleigh, helped me unpack. We hung all the clothes I had borrowed on huge rolling racks in the converted garage that I used as my office space. While she worked on having everything cleaned and returned, I focused on the hundreds of photos I had to go through, writing blog posts, responding to comments and emails, and sending gifts to the people who had invited me to shows. This time, I made sure to order the sweater I'd been wearing to be sent to Natasha at Chanel.

In the behind-the-scenes grind, I was fully at home and in my element. It felt meditative to sit at my desk wearing sweats, listening to music, and designing a page in Photoshop, tuning out the rest of my thoughts and the rest of the world. People assume that if you have ADHD it means you can't concentrate, which can be true. But it can also lead to hyper-focus and hyperconcentration in the right environment.

Yes, I was busy. Yes, I have ADHD. But, of course, there was more to the fact that I chose to dive headfirst into work before reconnecting with my husband. My emotions at the end of that trip were overwhelming—my disappointment about the flowers, my loneliness and insecurities throughout the trip, how hurt I was that Grant wasn't available to talk to me after the Dior show—and I didn't know how to face them. So, I did what I always did: I hid, I escaped, and I stuffed those emotions as far down as I possibly could. I kept the filter on my life because it felt safer and more comfortable to me than taking a look at what it was hiding.

At some point every night, Grant came out to the garage with dinner on a tray. I was so focused that I never would have remembered to eat if he hadn't literally put food in front of me. And then he returned to the house while I ate alone in front of my computer. After a few nights, I felt bad that we weren't spending more time together, so I ventured inside at dinnertime and poured us each a glass of wine.

"How was your day?" I asked Grant as we ate.

"It was fine. Same ole, same ole," he said. "Dealing with the annoying red tape of pulling permits on this Venice property."

I nodded and thought about what I could share with him about my time in New York and Paris, stretching my mind to think of something he would find interesting as I poked at my pasta with my fork.

"Oh," I said, "remember Tina, who came over here a few weeks ago? She acted like she didn't even really know me at Dior."

"Hmm," Grant said, trying to remember. "That sucks. The blonde?"

"No, you're thinking of Stephanie," I said. "It doesn't matter. I'm just being silly."

He looked at me, appearing a little confused, but I quickly got up and carried our plates into the kitchen. "I think I'll take a bath," I called to him from the other room. The conversation felt empty, and it was easier to just walk away than to try to figure out why.

Besides work, my favorite excuse to be alone and escape from real life was to take a bath. When I was done, I sat and waited as the water peeled away from my skin and slowly sank toward the great abyss below, letting out a big exhalation to release all my worries and hope that they would also slide their way down the drain. Sometimes it felt like a decade had passed before the tub was fully empty. But I found myself sitting there for a few extra minutes, dreading stepping back out and into my reality.

By the time I was done with my bath, Grant was in bed. I slipped into pajamas and sat at the kitchen table, scrolling through emails. I spent a few minutes clicking through all my open tabs and switching from task to task, and then leaned back in my chair, feeling a little frustrated and unfocused.

Out of the kitchen window, the clear, starry sky caught my attention. As always, I thought of my dad. But this time, when I located the brightest star I could find, I made a new wish: to live a life that I didn't feel the need to escape from.

2

The Farm Mouse and the City Mouse

Fifteen Years Earlier

AT TIMES, GROWING UP AS THE DAUGHTER OF A COTTON farmer was idyllic. I remember skipping school in the third grade to drive tractors all day. I remember spending afternoons chasing hogs and building tree houses with my brother. I remember how everything on the farm was a prop for a real or imagined adventure. The pigs were Oompa-Loompas, the picnic table was a spaceship, the back of my dad's pickup truck was a stage, and the dogs were my audience.

But as the years passed, my label shifted from being the daughter of a cotton farmer to the daughter of an alcoholic, and my ability to suspend reality and keep my child-like spirit alive became very, very difficult. I don't know why or how his drinking spiraled out of control, but by the time I was a young teen and my brother had left for college, my dad was drinking at least one liter of vodka each and every day. Sometimes, he'd crack open a second to get a head start on tomorrow.

Until then, my dad had always been able to function fairly well, but eventually his drinking caught up with him and started to cause errors in his judgment. One time, he was deep-frying shrimp and accidentally let the handle slip, spilling deathly hot grease on the garage floor. He often came home with pieces of his fingers missing, towels wrapped around the bloody cuts and duct tape holding the wounds closed. Our financial situation, which had always been tenuous and dependent on that season's crop, went downhill as well, as my dad neglected his bookkeeping and made reckless decisions. Eventually, he was on the brink of bankruptcy, and we were at risk of losing everything.

And so, my parents fought. These weren't the typical arguments that I imagine took place in every household. They dragged on for hours, and I mean *hours*—a steady flow of insults, passive-aggressive remarks, old resentments dragged up from the past, and full-blown screaming matches. Once we had all reached our exhaustion point, we retreated to our separate quarters: my dad in the master bedroom, my mom in my brother's room, and me in my room.

These fights started off between my mom and my dad, but over time I found myself acting as a mediator in their battles. For years, I'd seen the pain in my mom's eyes when she looked at my dad. I heard the anger in her voice when she spoke to him. I hurt for her, and I was filled with my own pain and anger and disappointment, too. So, I went to battle for her, with her, as we desperately tried to convince, inspire, motivate, and beg my dad to stop drinking. It became our entire lives' mission, with our self-esteem and emotions completely reliant on him and his actions. If he came home drunk or set the kitchen on fire, we were worthless wrecks. But if he was sober enough to attend one of my swim meets, which happened rarely, we were temporarily buoyed.

Without realizing it or even knowing what it meant, my mom and I had both slipped into full-blown codependency with my dad and with each other. My purpose was to protect my mom from my dad's words, motivate and educate my dad so that he would stop drinking, and to cover up the mess at home by desperately trying to control whatever I could. My needs were constantly put aside in favor of my parents' needs, and I worried about their emotional, physical, and mental well-being far more than I cared about my own.

Codependency leads to unhealthy coping behaviors in all of the involved parties, not just the addict. While my dad drank, shopping became a drug for me and my mom. We just needed an excuse to get out of the house and mask how we really felt. No one straight-out told me that if I wore a pretty enough dress, people wouldn't see the sadness in my eyes. But whenever we left the house, we put up an impressive facade, appearing to be a happy family in perfect, highly coordinated outfits.

This fit in seamlessly with the idealistic standards of my school and hometown, and I wore myself out trying to maintain this image of perfection, not just in what I wore but in all that I achieved. In high school, I was an all-state swimmer, cheerleader, and Miss Corpus Christi Teen. The intense football culture of South Texas was rooted in passion and obsessive pride. With gigantic jumbotrons lining the football fields, the entire town shut down on Friday nights so fans could pack the stadium, rain or shine, and cheer for our team. In my hometown, winning was not everything; it was the only thing. Being a cheerleader meant being a part of that high standard, and this competitive spirit bled into other sports, extracurricular activities, grades, who I dated, and even how many patches I had on my varsity jacket.

My mom and dad had both grown up in that same town, where everyone knew everyone. The idea of perfectionism was not just my mom's way of masking what was happening in our home; it was a part of the culture in general, and the pressure to keep up was intense. Before a party or event, I often caught my mom scolding herself in front of the mirror, saying things like "fucking idiot" or "stupid lipstick." The more stressful things got, the more my mom obsessed over a hair being out of place. The more my dad drank, the more my mom worried about a shoelace being untied.

I didn't tell anyone what my life was like at home. I didn't know the words, and I didn't think anyone would believe me. After all, everyone in Texas drank. Fighting was normal between parents. It was impossible to explain the intricate dynamic between my parents, their fights, and the role I played. Plus, what would it say about me if people knew the truth? It was easier to pretend that everything was perfect, mask my pain, and stuff my feelings down until I was so numb that I couldn't feel anything at all.

By my senior year of high school, my dad couldn't make it to 7:00 a.m. without his vodka. He wanted to quit, but he couldn't. His body wouldn't let him. Each morning when he woke up, withdrawal symptoms slowly set in. Hands shaking, sweating, vomiting, until he desperately reached for a bottle.

When I was a little girl, I wanted to escape into a world of make-believe. When I grew into my adolescence, I constantly entertained fantasies of running away and what life would be like in various exotic locales. I lived for these fantasies, for this land of make-believe, because hope of a better life somewhere else was all I had. The present was too painful, so I dreamed of escaping to a place far, far away. Little did I know that I couldn't escape from the impact that my reality had on me. It would follow me wherever I went until I learned to face it and truly heal.

On the morning I left for college, I peeked out from under the covers and looked at the alarm clock on my nightstand. It was 3:00 a.m., and I hadn't slept at all. The conflicting and confusing emotions I was feeling had kept me wide-awake all night. Ever since I was little, I suffered from intense separation anxiety when my parents left Justin and me for even a short amount of time. But I had also spent years fantasizing about the moment when I would finally break free from small-town Texas and the mess of my home life.

Now that the moment had finally arrived and I was moving over a thousand miles away, I was in a state of panic. Would there really be a place for a small-town girl like me in the big city of Chicago? Could I actually survive this far away from my family? And worst of all, what if the world out there didn't turn out to be any better than it was back here?

I reached for the landline I had gotten a few years before, back when I'd started high school. My very own phone number and extension. From maybe twenty feet away, I called my parents on the separate extension in their room.

"Jace? You okay?" Of course, my mother knew it was me.

"Will you come sleep with me?" I asked in a small voice. She was silent, but it was as if I could hear her nodding from the other room.

"Coming," she finally said.

For the next few hours, my mom scratched my back as I cried, just like she had when I was a toddler. By the time the alarm went off, my tears had dried, and I was ready to go. I was already adept at putting on a facade and hiding my true feelings, even from myself.

The little-used Audi my dad had gotten me was completely packed without an inch to spare when he came into the kitchen with a huge Tupperware bin that was labeled Survival Kit. It contained matches, flares, bottled water, crackers, candles, and detailed instructions on what to do in the event that I got stuck in a snow or ice storm. I re-arranged a few things to make room for it in the car, and then hugged him tight while avoiding his eyes. Then my mom and I climbed in the front seats and began the two-day drive from South Texas to Chicago. It was bittersweet to drive past my family's cotton fields for what would be the last time for a while. I was already homesick. But, ultimately, I knew that I needed to push past that feeling and break free.

To stop myself from crying, I tried to focus my thoughts on where I was going instead of what I was leaving behind. When I'd visited my aunt Celeste, my dad's sister, in Chicago the year before, I had immediately fallen in love. Chicago was so different from my home in South Texas in every possible way: the raw, real people, the cool air, the amazing food, the cool fashion, and the brownstone houses in Lincoln Park. And to me, that was the whole point. If I was going to run, I wanted to run far, to the opposite end of the earth, and to me, that meant Chicago.

My aunt Celeste owned a high-end clothing boutique that I absolutely loved. Before visiting her store, I had never seen high-end designer clothes in person. They were all so beautiful, and she organized the clothes so that it looked like the world's most exquisite closet. I loved spending time there, poring through the gorgeous cuts and fabrics and hanging out with my aunt Celeste. She was the cool aunt who knew everything about Chicago, from fashion to restaurants and the best places to visit in the city. During my visit, we'd wandered onto the DePaul University campus, and I felt in my gut that it was exactly where I needed to be.

But after we finally arrived and my mom helped settle me into the dorm before getting on a flight back to Texas, I wasn't so sure. I felt like I was floating adrift and was wholly unprepared for this new level of independence. There were basic things I was lacking, like a warm winter coat, socks, and boots. The only coat I owned was a lightweight suede jacket I had bought at Abercrombie & Fitch during my last shopping trip at the mall with my mom before I left for school. I loved that jacket. When I wore it, I thought I looked like the girl from *Almost Famous*—confident and aloof. But it was only lightly lined with faux fur and was the worst possible outerwear for Chicago's harsh winter weather. By October, my dorm mates were starting to wonder where my coat was.

The truth was that I couldn't afford to buy a new one. I was at DePaul on a combination of grants, loans, and cash I had saved up from waitressing the previous summer and from swindling my dad out of lunch money my entire senior year. But more than clothes or money, I was lacking the basic skills to thrive in this new environment. As far as I was from my family geographically, I had no separation from them emotionally. From afar, I still managed to get involved in my parents' fights, just as I had back home, always taking my mom's side and defending her against my dad.

I spoke to my mom multiple times each day and to my dad nearly as often. He tried to quit drinking in spurts, but could never sustain it, and he often moaned to me about how hard it was and how badly he wanted to quit but that he simply couldn't. Somehow, I always felt like his addiction was my fault, and my self-esteem was still completely dependent on him and his actions. I'd hang up after those calls and sit on the bed in my dorm room for hours, just staring out the window.

I had been assigned a dorm room with two roommates and felt incredibly anxious about living in such close quarters with other people. I don't remember ever sleeping that year. Back home, our closest neighbors were seven miles away, and we were intensely private. I never so much as slept over at a friend's house. Now I was living in a tiny dorm room with two strangers, listening to people run up and down the halls all night, terrified that someone would break into my dorm room while I was at class or, worse, trying to sleep.

After a few months, my anxiety and insomnia grew so intense that I put in a request to move off campus into a studio apartment. I also started seeing a college psychologist, who recommended that I take the antidepressant Lexapro. I didn't like the zoned-out way it made me feel, so in December I moved into my own tiny studio with no tools to help me cope.

I went through the motions. I joined a sorority, Delta Zeta, but didn't get too involved in their activities. I found a boyfriend, Tom, and treated him horribly, unconsciously replicating the unhealthy patterns I'd absorbed from my parents' marriage. Without constant fighting and drama around me, it felt like something was missing. Don't get me wrong; I didn't like the fighting. I hated how it made me feel scared and helpless. But when my parents fought,

I got an adrenaline rush, and over time, my body literally became addicted to that chemical release.

This is common among people who grow up with a lot of chaos and fear, and it can create unhealthy cycles of trauma throughout generations if true healing does not take place. For me, feeling threatened was sadly comfortable and stability felt boring and flat, leaving me craving an adrenaline high any way I could get it.

One night, I decided I was mad at Tom for smoking a cigarette in my apartment and made him sit in his car outside my dorm to prove how sorry he was. "If you go home," I told him, "we're done." I looked out the window at him sitting in his car in the freezing cold, like a puppy dog. God, I was such a bitch. After four hours, Tom was asleep and I felt he'd proved himself, so I finally let him back in. It took me years to realize that I was trying to push him away to prove that he didn't really love me. I wanted to be right so much more than I wanted to be happy.

I'm not sure if things between my mom and dad quickly devolved after I left, or if it just became clear to my mom how bad it really was without me there to support her and intervene. For six years, I had spent every single day begging my dad to stop drinking. The rest of the time, I used every ounce of energy I had trying to be the perfect daughter so he wouldn't have an excuse to drink. I hid bottles. I bargained with him. I manipulated. I fought. I pleaded. I loved my dad more than anything, but I just couldn't do it anymore.

After being at college for only a couple of months, I cut off contact with my dad, and started ignoring his calls and emails. It was the hardest thing I'd ever done, but talking to him always made me feel worse, not better, so the pain of not speaking to him came with a tiny bit of relief.

I continued to talk to my mom multiple times a day. She was in a panic because, on top of everything else, our finances were in ruin. My mom wanted to plan an intervention, and I agreed to fly home for it, even though I was feeling resentful and pessimistic. I'd been begging my dad to stop drinking for years, and I didn't see how this would suddenly change anything. It was all so dramatic. The cliché of nearly losing the farm, the intervention, all of it. I responded by trying to bury my emotions as much as possible and just keep floating.

In high school, I always did my homework, took every test seriously, crossed all of my *t*'s, and dotted each and every *i*. Because of my ADHD, I couldn't concentrate in crowded rooms and was allowed to take all my tests out in the hallway. My dad never cared about grades. He always told me, "Just pass," but deep down, I thought that if I did well in school, he'd have one less reason to drink. Of course, the pressure I put on myself made my ADHD symptoms even worse.

In college, I finally accepted the fact that there was truly nothing I could do to stop my dad from drinking. I felt better mentally when I took the pressure off myself and stopped worrying about grades. But I still had bad days when my deep-rooted perfectionist and competitive habits kicked in, with the anxiety that went along with them.

On those days, I felt paralyzed. The classroom was too

hot or too cold. The tiny noise of a classmate tapping a pencil flooded my mind, muting out whatever the professor was saying. History was all out of order, with the dates all jumbled on the whiteboard. None of it made sense to me, and no matter how hard I tried, I couldn't focus. And the more confused I got, the more anxious I felt, and the stronger my ADHD symptoms kicked in. Thousands of thoughts raced through my mind so quickly that I couldn't hold on to any of them. My brain felt like the fuzzy radio frequency between channels.

These feelings followed me from the classroom to conversations with my peers. My body was always there, but my mind was elsewhere, unable to speak and finding it even harder to listen. It felt like I was wearing noise-canceling headphones, and instead of the conversation I was allegedly having, all I could focus on was devastating what-if scenarios that suddenly popped into my mind. What if that car drove onto campus, broke through the library, and crashed into our table? I ran through game plans in my mind about what I would do to save our lives in each horrible far-fetched scenario. I did this over and over and over again while my classmates talked about weekend plans. I couldn't hear them.

I tried to pretend that everything was fine, but behind my facade, I doubted myself and was too ashamed to even try to explain the internal battles I was facing. I hardly understood them myself and just wanted to be a normal college girl. But inside I felt like a fraud.

It wasn't until much later in life that I learned how to use my ADHD as my superpower. When I hyper-focus on a specific task, person, or thing that I care about, I can work faster and more effectively than my neurotypical peers. Because my mind is so creative, I'm able to think of outside-of-the-box scenarios and problem solve much faster than most people. And because I know I'm fighting an uphill battle in some situations, I always try to work harder than everyone else. My struggle eventually became my motivator and my recipe for success.

During this time, I began writing about my home life in my creative writing classes. Writing served as the perfect outlet for me to express my post-trauma stress, and I laid out all my stories on the page for my professors to dissect. There was the one about a fishing trip I took with my dad when I was nine years old and he let me drink Miller Lite as long as I promised to keep it a secret from my mom. There was the story of my dad torching the lawn mower with gas in a drunken rage. The story of my dad flooding the kitchen because he left a dishrag in the sink and the water turned on. There was a series of short stories outlining the many nights I had to help my dad walk out of restaurants to the truck so that I could drive him home safely (long before I had a license). Then there was the story about how he stumbled into my high school graduation ceremony drunk, in front of all my classmates. It was the first time anyone from outside of my family got even a glimpse of what was really going on at home.

After hiding the tearful stories and my conflicting emotions toward my dad's alcoholism for so many years, it was such a relief to type out a grand purge of stories and feelings. My professors were incredibly supportive of my writing, and always encouraging me to dig deeper in my storytelling. I didn't realize how much I needed my feelings to be validated or to hear that just because my dad was living a messed-up life, it didn't mean that I had to live the same way or that I was messed up, too.

On the flight home for the intervention, my pulse quickened and tears suddenly pricked at my eyes as we climbed toward the sky. "I still get scared at takeoff sometimes, too," the kind-looking older woman sitting next to me said, handing me a tissue. *How embarrassing.* I just nodded, wiping my eyes. I didn't have the words to tell her that it was so much more than a simple fear of flying.

The intervention itself felt like such a cliché, like a movie script. It was exactly what you would picture. We all sat across from our addict family member, playing our roles. "When you did *X*, it made me feel *Y*." When it was my turn, I said, "When you couldn't stay sober until 7:00 a.m., it made me feel sad." What I really wanted to say was, *When you completely abandoned me as a role model, it made me question who I was as a person and laid the foundation for a lifetime of trust issues.* But I did what I do best and played the part, read the script, and listened to the rules.

After the intervention, I was shocked when my dad reluctantly agreed to go to rehab for thirty days. He, of course, went kicking and screaming like a little baby with his bottle in hand. I went back to school and then flew back down to Texas a month later for family day at the rehab center, which was like his graduation.

On family day, my mom and I saw the hospital-like

quarters my dad had been staying in and attended family therapy together. Everyone was putting on a cheery face and walking on eggshells, and it made me nauseous. I sat in the cold metal folding chair with my arms folded across my chest, picking at the worn denim of my jacket as the therapist asked me to tell my dad how his drinking made me feel. The question infuriated me. Seriously? How did she think it made me feel?

"He already knows," I told her. "I've been telling him for years."

"Try telling him again," she said patiently.

Okay. Fine.

"I felt hurt," I said plainly. "It hurt that you always chose alcohol over me."

"I'm sorry, Jace," my dad said, his normally booming voice dimmed. "It's going to be different now. You'll see."

I looked in my dad's eyes for the first time in months. I had been avoiding making eye contact because on some level I knew what I would see in his eyes: the fact that I couldn't believe him. "Okay, prove it," I told him, quickly looking away. I knew he wouldn't. Not because he didn't want to, but because he couldn't. He wasn't ready. For once, I desperately wished I were wrong.

But I wasn't. I went back to school, and my mom kept me posted on everything that was going on at home. My dad stayed sober for maybe a month before he started drinking nonalcoholic beer. Then he quickly switched back to regular beer, with vodka close behind. Less than three months after the intervention, he was right back where he'd started.

★ ★ ★

The sorority I joined was always holding retreats and events. I attended many of them, though I often remained on the sidelines. I had a huge wall up, felt completely disconnected, and honestly didn't know how to have a group of girlfriends, so I tended to play the shy card. This was really because of how scared I was to open up to anyone. As a child, anytime I allowed myself to be vulnerable and begged my dad to stop drinking, he didn't quit. My childhood brain interpreted this as him rejecting and abandoning me. So, to me, at this time in my life, opening up meant getting hurt. It was safer to push people away when it felt like they were getting too close.

On top of that, other girls my age intimidated me. They seemed to have it all together, and I had no idea where they'd learned to do life with such carefree confidence. The girls in my sorority were outgoing, funny, and self-assured. I could fake those things, but inside I felt insecure and terrified of getting hurt. So, I figured I'd just protect myself by keeping my guard up.

From afar, I admired one group of girls in particular: Shannon, Gia, and Stefanie. They had been a clique since the beginning of freshman year and were always the first ones to jump at volunteer or committee work. They had private jokes between them and shared a fun, outgoing energy that I couldn't help but notice. I watched this group of girls who really seemed to like and support each other with a mix of dismay and envy.

The summer after my freshman year, we went on a retreat to one of the senior girls' family lake house. The first night, we held a candlelight circle. It was a perfect, breezy Chicago evening, and the worn Delta Zeta sweatshirt my "big sister" had handed down to me was enough to keep me warm. It was dark out by the lake, except for the tiny tea candles we each held and a small scattering of stars. We took turns going around the circle and sharing something that was weighing on us with the group. I tried to focus on listening to the other girls as a knot formed in my stomach. I knew what I had to share. It was the only thing that made any sense. But I had never spoken about my dad's drinking out loud. Not to anyone, never mind a group of girls who I longed to see me as someone who belonged.

By the time it was my turn, my heart was pounding. *Screw it*, I thought, and I just started talking. Staring down at my candle, with little emotion in my voice, I told them how much I had idolized my dad as a young girl. When he put me to bed, he'd always squeeze my hand three times to say *I love you*, and I'd squeeze back if I was still awake (which was rarely). Every morning before school, he went out to get me my favorite breakfast tacos. I hadn't realized at the time that this was the perfect excuse for him to start drinking vodka each morning during the drive.

I told them about my parents' fights, which escalated over the years as my dad's drinking got worse and worse. How by the time I was in high school, he was emotionally abusive to my mom, and I was the only one there to defend her. I told them about the intervention, the failed attempt at rehab, and how guilty I felt for being relieved when I wasn't speaking to him.

Then I told them about how the summer before college,

while I was waitressing tables to save money for school, my dad was trying his best to sober up on his own. After work one day, I walked into the house and found him unconscious and foaming at the mouth. He'd had a near-death seizure caused by alcohol withdrawal. I told them about how once my dad was settled into his hospital bed and hooked up to IV fluids, I sat on the edge of the bed and grabbed his fragile hand. I squeezed three times, our code for *I love you*. He didn't squeeze back.

When I was done, I looked up, expecting to see horror or disgust in the other girls' eyes. Instead, I saw tears. Growing up, my mom was very clear that we were to never ever speak about my dad's drinking to anyone. I assumed that people would immediately reject me if they knew the truth, that I was nothing more than a dumb little farm girl with an alcoholic dad. But what my sorority sisters met me with instead was acceptance. Support. Understanding. It was more than I ever could have hoped for. I had truly never believed that I could tell the truth about myself and still be accepted.

The next morning, we were sitting around the living room, talking. Shannon, Gia, and Stefanie had gotten an apartment-style dorm on campus for the next semester and were looking for one more roommate. "Does anyone still need a place to live?" Gia asked the group.

I hadn't figured out my living situation yet for the next year. This was one of the many adult responsibilities in college that I found completely overwhelming. Yet I was hesitant to say something because I wasn't sure if they'd really want to room with me. They went around and asked a couple of the other girls, and then Gia's eyes landed on me. "What about you, Jacey?" she asked.

"Yeah, actually, that might work out well," I told her.

"Awesome!" Shannon said, and all three girls crossed the room to give me a hug and take a picture together, commemorating the fact that we were going to be roommates. I was used to plastering on a fake smile for pictures, but when I look back at that picture even now, I can tell how authentic it was, how happy I felt to be accepted and welcomed into their circle.

My life did a complete one-eighty that year, and not just because of my new roommates. It was around this same time that my mom finally decided to leave my dad. During my freshman year, I called her every single day and encouraged her to leave him. Of course, I wished my parents could have made it work, but I knew how much better off my mom would be without my dad. When she told me that he was still hitting the bottle at 8:00 a.m. and ending the day screaming at her, I worried for her and felt guilty for leaving her behind. I wanted her to escape just like I had, and she had finally set herself free.

My mom had always talked about pursuing her master's degree in music education. She was a talented musician, but had put her career aside when she married my dad. When I was growing up, she repeatedly told me to never do the same thing. As my brother and I got older, she returned to music and ended up teaching in my middle school. Now she was leaving Texas for the first time and enrolled at none other than…DePaul University.

That's right—my school. At the beginning of my sophomore year, I drove all the way home in my Audi to pick up my mom. I was only in Texas for a few days and managed to barely interact with my dad. He was busy avoiding my mom and me by driving around the fields to *check on crops* and, of course, drinking.

After we packed up the Audi and a U-Haul with my mom's belongings, I brought her back to Chicago with me, and settled her into an apartment instead of the other way around. Have you seen the movie *Life of the Party*, where Melissa McCarthy plays a mom who follows her daughter to college? That was basically my life.

Even more than having my mom close by, living with Shannon, Gia, and Stefanie was a game changer. I'm not exaggerating when I say that those girls saved my life. Little by little, I was able to let my guard down around them. They were fun and open and taught me what it meant to be a good girlfriend. No matter how well they got to know me, they never rejected or abandoned me. Over time, this helped me slowly begin to trust.

To make money, I picked up shifts at my aunt Celeste's boutique. I loved working there. Not only was her store located within walking distance to campus, but it was a popular boutique that everyone in Chicago knew. She was even featured on *The Oprah Winfrey Show*! I learned so much from watching my aunt Celeste work with customers and help them style things together, but mainly there were two key takeaways from my job there: 1. the art of the style, and 2. the art of the sell.

The art of the style doesn't come overnight. While I nervously picked my nails behind the cashier's desk, a habit whenever I'm feeling excited or anxious, Celeste made her way around the store, selecting garment after garment to style a mannequin in the front window. "It's all about the windows," she told me. "We need them to really draw the customers in."

I watched Celeste pull a very simple white button-down top that looked pretty ordinary on the rack and put it under a tan blazer with black trousers. She rolled the cuff of the white button-down over the sleeve of the blazer and popped the white collar out from the top. She then buttoned the neck all the way up to the top and put a necklace around the neck.

I watched her closely as she stepped back to admire her work. I thought it looked great, but she shook her head and stripped down the mannequin, clearly disappointed. "Too stuffy," she said. Then she went to the front racks and grabbed a chunky navy blue cable-knit sweater from the newest Theory collection. As she passed through the middle of the store, she swiftly pulled a navy, maroon, and ivory wool plaid skirt by Nanette Lepore. She tossed the navy sweater over the white button-down and left a few of the bottom buttons open as she tucked half of the shirt into the skirt.

"See? It's fall! And this way the shirt looks more effortless, like the girl slept in it. It just feels better, don't you think?"

I was in awe. How did Celeste know how to do that? Was there some special school I could enroll in to gain her eye for style? I would have given anything to learn all the insider tricks that seemed to come so naturally to her.

When it came to the art of the sell, Celeste was also the queen. When someone came in, she smiled at them but hung back instead of immediately bombarding them. She reminded me how annoying it was when a customer walked into a store and it was obvious that the salesclerks were working on commission. Celeste had all the employees split their commissions, so it was more of a collaborative effort and less of a hustle to sell our customers on clothing. After a few moments, she'd make a comment about the weather or a popular TV show to open up a conversation, and before you knew it, the customer was checking out with a sale of over two thousand dollars.

When she wasn't working, Celeste was quiet and standoffish, which made her words carry even more weight. I eagerly sought her approval. "You did well," she told me at the end of my first shift, her fingers fiddling in her lap. "But why are you wearing so much black eyeliner? You're so pretty with no makeup. Don't you feel better without all that crap on your face?"

I never wore black eyeliner again.

After working at Celeste's for just a few months, there was a customer in the store who was trying on a light blue sundress. I watched her twisting in front of the full-length mirror, clearly undecided about whether or not she liked how she looked in the dress.

"I saw another customer buy that yesterday for a bridal shower," I told her with a smile. "It looked so good on her, too." She continued looking in the mirror, appearing unsure. "You could also wear it with a blazer," I said, putting down the stack of sweaters I was holding. "Let me get one for you. I also saw someone wear it with a shirt underneath. I'll grab you one of those, too."

Yes, she bought the dress. But the most important thing I learned was that it wasn't about the garment she was buying. It was about how she felt when she was wearing it and finding the right accessories that helped her feel the way she wanted to. Experimenting with Celeste's merchandise, I found that different brands and styles evoked completely different feelings in myself. I loved the rush I got when I tried on the designer labels I couldn't afford to buy. Ralph Lauren made me feel classic, preppy, and pretty. Tory Burch made me feel current, stylish, and strong. Bebe made me feel excited, ready to dance, and young. BCBG made me feel trendy, cool, and carefree. I was hooked on these different feelings that I could score just by getting dressed. Celeste showed customers how to style outfits and sold them new pieces of their wardrobe. But much more important, she introduced her customers and me to the way different outfits can make you feel. Helping these women feel better about themselves made me feel better about myself in return, and this idea of dressing for the way you want to feel eventually became the concept behind my entire brand.

One night, I closed my shift at Celeste's and walked back to the apartment, where my girlfriends were waiting for me. It was one of the first spring evenings that was warm enough for me to enjoy walking outside. Armitage Avenue was bustling with tourists and college students, and the wind carried the sounds of laughter across the city. As I walked past the rows of brownstones, I finally reached the window to our apartment and stopped to look in.

I peered in the window, watching my friends gather around the kitchen table, setting up for our weekly tradition, Champagne Thursday. Shannon was wearing a capped-sleeve black cocktail dress with a bold red lip as she placed a tray of cheese onto the table. Gia stood at the end of the table, talking animatedly, her hands just as wild as her beautiful black curly hair. Stefanie was just a few feet behind them, pouring flutes of champagne in a black silk dress with a blazer on top. They all had smiles on their faces. And a huge smile spread across my face as well, as I experienced a completely new version of "home."

3

First Bitten

DESPITE HAVING SUCH WONDERFUL FRIENDS, A FULFILLING job at Celeste's, and even my mom nearby, the ground in Chicago never felt completely solid underneath my feet. My parents were in the middle of a divorce and filing for bankruptcy, making my financial situation beyond precarious. I never knew whether or not I'd be able to pay my next tuition bill or for my next meal, and my credit card debt was spiraling out of control.

I had to go to Western Union to cash my checks because my bank account was so overdrawn, which meant waiting in line in the cold and giving up a significant percentage of my earnings. Other times, I wrote hot checks to Chicago's Pizza just to eat and then had to pay the overdraft fee, which cost more than the pizza, when they bounced. Then the next day when I got hungry I did the same thing again or just ate a ninety-nine-cent can of ravioli soup from the 7-Eleven down the street. I attended financial-aid meetings weekly, and every time my tuition bill was due I seriously wondered if I was going to have to drop out of school.

In between all this, I floated through sorority events, work shifts, spending time with my mom, and a truly half-assed academic performance. I was concerned about my dad, who was still drinking, and I worried about what would happen to him if he lost the farm. My dad loved farming. It was his joy in life, and I never once heard him complain about going to work because it didn't feel like a job to him at all. But his drinking led to poor management of the bookkeeping involved in running the farming business. In addition to the actual planting and harvesting, being a cotton farmer meant being responsible for the millions of dollars' worth of tractors and other farming equipment that we rented during harvest season, filing paperwork with the bank and the USDA each year, and keeping an eye on the cotton-farming industry trends and market.

On top of all that, many local landowners hired my dad to farm their land, too. He was responsible for planting and harvesting their cotton crops from start to finish, budgeting, invoicing, etc. All of these things had been slipping more and more each year. The more my dad drank, the further downhill his finances went. Now he was in real trouble.

We didn't know it at the time, but there was a guardian angel looking over us. One of the people who had hired my dad to farm her land for years was Mrs. Lang, a very kind older woman. When I was a child, she was one of the only women in South Texas to run her own farm. And when Mrs. Lang could no longer do it all on her own, she hired my dad to farm the land for her. She loved my dad, and our family had a close relationship with Mrs. Lang until she passed away when I was in middle school.

Mrs. Lang was devoutly religious. In her will, she left her land to the evangelical Christian minister Billy Graham. But he was contractually obligated to sell it to my dad at a low rate over a ten-year period. So, we now owned Mrs. Lang's farm in exchange for monthly payments to Billy Graham and his church. A few years after she passed away, when I was in high school, my parents relocated Mrs. Lang's old farmhouse and built a new one that we moved into exactly where her house had stood. In addition to our own family farm, the Lang farm and the house were some of the assets that we were now in danger of losing.

I wish I could remember where I was when I found out that an oil company that was scouting in our area had discovered a natural gas well under Mrs. Lang's farm. They had been fracking the South Texas area for years, but tended to fall short when it came to scoring big. When the bigwigs from the oil company came to town, people noticed. All of the farmers buzzed with gossip about whose farm was being investigated for oil and gas. Now that gossip was about us.

It wasn't like in *The Beverly Hillbillies* where you strike oil and become rich overnight. The news trickled in over months during my sophomore year of college, but the reality of what it meant for my family didn't truly hit for years. There was no one dramatic movie moment or phone call saying, "Your life has changed." At first, all we knew was that the oil company had found natural gas. We had no idea that it would end up being the biggest strike in our county's history.

Even once we knew it was significant, we still weren't sure who owned the oil and mineral rights to the land, my dad or Billy Graham. The lawyers spent some time fighting over it, but in the end, it wasn't much of a gray area at all. In her will, Mrs. Lang had specifically left the oil and mineral rights to my dad. Any money stemming from that natural gas would go directly to us.

Even then, my parents refused to believe that any of this was real until there was money in the bank. Like many families that struggle with addiction, mine was big on secrets, so my parents insisted on keeping the whole thing as quiet as possible. We had groomed ourselves so carefully to keep my dad's drinking a secret that we resisted sharing any news with family or friends. Everything was a secret—the good, the bad, and the ugly. If we shared good news and allowed others into our "inner circle," they would likely ask more questions. It was easier to just shut people out completely and keep things nice and tidy. This was one reason that I never had any real friends until college. So, nobody else knew about the gas strike, and I didn't know what to make of it.

Nothing in my life changed except for a vague notion

that money might not be a constant struggle anymore. We were never going to be as rich as *The Beverly Hillbillies*, but we could keep our land, avoid bankruptcy, and pay off our significant debts. In the end, I received very little of that money, but it did help me stay in school. By the time it started to roll in, I was self-sufficient and supporting myself without much help from my parents.

The oil money wasn't just a relief for my dad, my brother, and me. Even though my parents were going through a divorce, they still cared a lot about each other, and my dad wasn't going to keep my mom from her fair share. While getting her degree, my mom had been working two jobs in Chicago. During the day, she taught at a mid-city school, and on weekends she worked as a sales associate in the Macy's shoe department. She was barely making ends meet and running herself into the ground.

As the news of an oil strike trickled in during the months leading up to my twenty-first birthday, my roommates and I were saving up for a trip to celebrate. Now I could go without guilt or stress about my ever-increasing debt.

Growing up, we only took a handful of family trips that I can remember, and they were always within driving distance because we couldn't afford to fly. During the year, we spent our Saturday evenings gathered on a blanket in the living room, collecting all our spare change and rolling the coins. This was our travel fund for a trip to Ruidoso, New Mexico, where my dad went elk hunting and took Justin and me treasure hunting. An eccentric billionaire named Forrest Fenn claimed to have buried a real live treasure chest in the Rocky Mountains. On horseback, we explored caves and mountains, searching in vain for the buried treasure.

When I had outgrown treasure hunting at fifteen, our family went treasure hunting in Las Vegas for the first time. I loved the casinos, and while my parents gambled, I kept sneaking away to play slots illegally. But I got a rush from the thrill of the roulette table in particular. For me, there was a romance to the fast and furious play of roulette. I loved the endless variations and the fact that anyone, no matter who they were or where they came from, could learn how to play quickly and successfully.

So, when it came time to pick a place for a trip with my college girlfriends, we decided on Las Vegas. The girls and I settled into the Paris hotel and got all dolled up in our fanciest little black Bebe strapless dresses and sky-high heels before heading down to the casino floor. It was bustling and smoky, and I could smell the vodka that stuck to the drapes, the floor, and the dark green felt that dressed the gambling tables. The roulette table sat at the end of the only two rows of tables on the main floor. It was perfectly positioned by a fountain, next to the cashier's station, and adjacent to the high-limit room. Shannon, Gia, and Stefanie wanted to play slot machines and blackjack, so we made a plan to rendezvous at the middle bar in an hour.

I pulled out the brown leather stool at the table, nodded to the pit boss to confirm it was empty, and laid two hundred-dollar bills down on the table. If I had learned anything from watching my parents gamble, it was to detach all emotion from the money I played with. Once I put down those bills, I considered it a purchase to enjoy one hour of gambling time. I never ever expected to win. I always focused on the fun at the table, the conversation with the dealer, and most important, the confident, easy-going energy I felt toward the room. When I was in Las Vegas, I was completely anonymous. No one knew anything about my background, or my family, or my secret insecurities. I could put on a dress and transform into a different, more confident version of myself.

After I had been sitting at the table for about an hour, my stack of chips was running low, and it was time to meet up with the girls. *Let's go all in*, I thought to myself. I took my chips and sprinkled them across the table like confetti, picking all my favorite numbers from birthdays to ages, all the way down to my favorite number, thirteen. Thirteen is considered an unlucky number, which was exactly why I loved it so much.

The dealer spun the roulette wheel with force as I continued placing my chips across the table. I noticed the other players following my moves. The wheel began to slow, and just before the dealer waved his hand across the board, indicating that all bets were closed, I placed a stack on black to back up my black-thirteen.

I sat back in the stool, looked up at the clock, and took a big sip from my vodka soda in the most nonchalant way possible. I had become very talented at putting up walls to mask my true emotions, so good that I often felt nothing but numbness as a result. I never watched the wheel because I believed it gave me luck, but I heard the slowing of the roulette wheel, the bouncing of the marker, and a loud cheer erupt from the table. I slowly took my eyes from the clock and, one by one, met the eyes of every single person at the table, cheering and looking at me. I smirked and looked down to see that black-thirteen had hit. It had hit big. I walked away from the table with ten times the two hundred dollars I had sat down with.

There was no question in my mind as to what I was going to do with my winnings. I wasn't back in Chicago for forty-eight hours before I was headed to Michigan Avenue to go shopping at Chanel.

A farm girl like me purchasing her first Chanel bag wasn't something that happened overnight. It took years of consideration, obsession, and succumbing to advertising. I had been pining over Chanel since my teenage years. When my mom and I looked through fashion magazines together, I remember seeing image after image of models and celebrities wearing the classic Chanel quilted flap bag. By the time I was in college, I was convinced that owning a Chanel bag meant I was elevated to a new status.

I didn't know this at the time, but there are marketing strategies in place to ensure that even someone like me who grew up on a farm still knows and covets the name Chanel. Back in 1974 when the Chanel No. 5 fragrance wasn't selling well, the CEO reduced its availability from eighteen thousand to twelve thousand units in the US and heavily invested in advertising the new limited quantity to instill the fear of missing out. They were decades ahead of the FOMO curve. Throughout the years, the brand made its limited availability an integral part of its business strategy.

Despite her humble beginnings as an underprivileged orphan with no formal schooling, Coco Chanel founded and pioneered the most legendary fashion house in the world, one that felt exclusive and highly in demand. I related to her story, and it inspired me to know that someone who had had such a difficult start in life had made it so big. Like Coco, I wanted to reach a higher status than the one I had grown up with.

Both my connection to Coco Chanel and my appetite for a higher status made my desire for a Chanel bag even greater. I felt that owning this designer handbag would be a sign to the world that I was succeeding in life. A Chanel bag was sleek, expensive, and beautiful on the outside, which was exactly how I wanted people to see me. I didn't want anyone to know that the inside of my Chanel bag was filled with gum wrappers, 7-Eleven receipts, and an empty wallet, or that inside I was just as much of a mess.

There have always been two Jaceys when it comes to fashion: Fashionista Jacey, who dresses to the nines, and Farm Girl Jacey in torn jeans with bare feet. Farm Girl Jacey wanted to believe that a bag was just a bag, and it didn't matter which one I carried. But Fashionista Jacey knew that a Chanel bag was like a membership card to a secret club of fashion insiders. I wanted to be in that club, to be the type of woman who I imagined carried a Chanel bag, even if deep down I knew that wasn't who I was. At least, not yet.

On the day of my shopping trip, I purposefully dressed a bit sloppy in ripped jeans from Target and my old worn jacket from Abercrombie & Fitch because I wanted to have my *Pretty Woman* moment. I imagined the judgmental faces of the saleswomen as I walked into the store, looking like I couldn't afford anything and then proving them all wrong by pulling out wads of cash. Inside, I still felt very much like a poor little farm girl. I didn't belong at Chanel. But I had the money for my purchase, so how did I belong any less than the other people shopping there?

This was the same feeling I had at the Dior fashion show in Paris all those years later, the sense that the people around me believed I didn't belong. They didn't always say it with words. Sometimes it was the way their eyes landed on me. Sometimes it came from inside, a feeling that I was standing in a doorway between where I'd already been and where I wanted to go. It was a lot easier in those moments to retract into the former shell of the person I once was. Pushing forward toward something bigger felt unnerving and scary. But as I've stood in those doorways throughout my life, something always tugged at me to just GO.

The doors opened to the Chanel store, and I felt a wave of heat slap me in the face. The bitter Chicago winter was still hanging on in April, and the stores were blasting heaters in the doorways as shoppers came in. I entered the store with single-minded focus. I knew exactly what I wanted: that quintessential quilted Chanel bag, with its chain strap and iconic logo. Though I had always preferred black to pink, I bought a pink bag in honor of my grandma Meme, who always told me that pink was timeless and fashionable. It was also the color that Mischa Barton's character wore on *The O.C.*, which was my favorite show at the time.

I took the bag from the salesgirl as if it were made of fine china and looked at myself in the full-length mirror as I carefully hooked the sparkling chain strap over my shoulder. The reflection of the metal somehow made my eyes appear to shine brighter. I noticed that I was standing a little straighter than normal, and especially how the bag instantly elevated my entire look, from the ripped jeans to the worn jacket to my messy blond hair. With the bag tying it all together, these haphazard choices all looked intentional and correct.

I didn't know then that true confidence runs a lot deeper than fancy clothes and pretty pictures. I naively believed that the bag could actually make me feel self-assured. In my reflection, and for a quick moment, I no longer felt like that scared and confused little farm girl. I was as self-assured and confident as Mischa Barton or Coco Chanel. I was in control. I belonged. And I was hooked.

A couple of months later, my mom and I flew home to Texas together for the Fourth of July. It was our first time back since Christmas. Though my dad had filed for divorce, my parents still put on a good face for holidays and family functions.

As the tiny puddle-jumper plane crossed above our cotton fields heading toward the Corpus Christi airport, I looked out my window and caught sight of something I had never seen before in South Texas: the oil company landing a giant helicopter on the Lang farm to look at the oil well. Disbelief washed over me as the plane passed directly over it. We never saw helicopters growing up, especially landing on a farm. I turned my neck back, squinting to see if I could spot my dad on the farm. We hadn't spoken in months, and just as I thought I saw him, a big fluffy cloud crept into my window, blocking my view.

Later that afternoon, we arrived home. The house my parents had built where Mrs. Lang's once stood represented a dark time in my family's history. We had moved in just as my dad's drinking had gotten completely out of control. While my original childhood home had often felt like a safe haven, this was a place of fear and loneliness. And now the helicopter and oil rig were beginning to make the farmland I had grown up on feel foreign to me, too.

Standing in the exact spot where Mrs. Lang's creaky front porch used to be, I watched the helicopter blades as they started to spin around and the men in suits climbed back on board for takeoff. Tiny green cotton plants were just starting to sprout, and dirt danced around in the distance. The helicopter flew farther and farther away, and with every breath I let out, the sun's rays grew dimmer. The day met dusk. I realized that as that sun was leaving our field in darkness, it was headed to light up another field somewhere else. I wanted to be on that field. I wanted to be anywhere but here.

When the sun rose the next morning, it was the third of July. My parents and I hung around the house for most of the day, with my mom and me drinking and enjoying getting a little tipsy to celebrate the holiday. The Fourth of July was always a big deal in Texas and we wanted to celebrate. I was aware of the fact that alcoholism was hereditary, but I knew I wasn't an alcoholic because while I liked drinking, I didn't need it. I was always careful not to let my drinking get out of control, but I felt safe enjoying alcohol in moderation.

When my dad got out of rehab the first time, my mom and I avoided drinking around him, but we were done coddling him, and he was drinking nonstop again anyway. At that point, my mom and I knew that he would keep drinking until he was good and ready to get sober, if and when that day ever came. There was nothing we could do or say to stop him. If there were, it would have already happened because we'd tried everything.

Over the course of the evening, a few family members came by. At first, I didn't think much of it. Most of my extended family lived close by and often popped in for a visit. But after a while, they began gathering very seriously in the living room, talking in hushed voices, and I wondered what was going on. My mom and I looked at each other with question marks on our faces. It was clear that she didn't know what was happening, either. Finally, my mom sat down next to my aunt Celeste. They had always been close. "What's going on?" she asked.

"We've arranged another intervention," Celeste replied matter-of-factly. My mom and I looked at each other again, this time in disbelief that they had gone ahead and planned this without including us.

I plopped down on the big red leather sofa in the living room and muttered to myself, "Good luck with that!" I stifled a nervous laugh as a familiar adrenaline rush pulsed through my body. I was certain that my dad would put on a big show, and that my relatives would finally understand what it really felt like to spend years and years trying and failing to get him to stop drinking.

To my astonishment, two hours later, my uncle was loading my dad into the car on our front driveway. My dad was fighting back tears with a handle of vodka in his hand, savoring every last sip of freedom before he checked in to another thirty days of rehab. My mom and I stood on our front porch and watched in disbelief as they drove away. I found out later that my dad drank that entire bottle of vodka on the ride to the rehab center. When he checked in, they told him that if he'd had one more sip, he would have died.

We went back to Chicago and then thirty days later my mom and I returned to the rehab center for another crack at family day. Once again, I was feeling angry and resentful, without one speck of hope that it would stick. Less than a year had passed since my dad's last stint in rehab. Why would this time be any different? But when my dad entered the room for family therapy, I could see right away that something *was* different. There was a change in the way he carried himself, and when I managed to look, there was something new in his eyes. I could see that he wanted it this time.

My mom and I had been right that we couldn't make him stay sober. In any case of addiction and recovery, the addict has to be the one to want it. I really don't know what changed between my dad's first attempt at rehab and his second. Maybe he finally realized that if he didn't sober up, he was actually going to die. Regardless, I could feel that something had shifted, and that allowed me to dare to do something I hadn't done in years—hope.

Once again, the therapist asked me to tell my dad how everything he'd done over the past several years had affected me. If she asked me this question now, I would say that growing up in a home that was fueled by alcoholism had bred a multitude of emotional issues and coping mechanisms. Because I never knew when my dad would show up at home or to an event drunk, I learned at an early age to think fast on my feet, which led me to make big decisions impulsively. In college, I quit my history class after one bad grade and bought that Chanel bag with my roulette winnings instead of setting that money aside for savings and school.

At the same time, my overdeveloped sense of responsibility for my parents and their relationship led me to take on too many projects at once and to always feel responsible for other people's problems. Later in life, I chronically took on too much at once, which left me feeling burnt-out but also fueled by the burnout. I took on other people's stress as my own, getting wrapped up in my friends' relationship and health problems. I thrived in the chaos and drama and excitement that I was used to from home, and replicated it in my own relationships. A simple and loving relationship felt dull to me because it lacked the instability and turmoil I craved. For me, chaos equaled stability and safety because that was the environment I had been groomed in. But I'd say that the number one way my dad's drinking affected me was by instilling a crippling fear of abandonment.

But at the time, I had just turned twenty-one and wasn't close to understanding or being able to articulate any of this yet. So, I simply rattled off a simplistic list of all the things my dad had said or done over the years that hurt my feelings. When I was finished, he went through my list one by one and apologized for every single thing. It's hard to explain, but as I listened to his apologies, I realized that I didn't want to be angry with him anymore. I had been angry for so long, and I was so tired of carrying it around with me.

We both wanted to quit. Whether my dad *deserved* it or not, the truth is that, just as he finally wanted to give up drinking, I finally wanted to forgive him, and needed to for my own well-being.

Then my dad presented me with a gift: a blue beaded necklace that he had made during an arts-and-crafts class in rehab. How can I say this kindly? It was not the kind of thing I would ever wear. It looked like something a child would make as a Mother's Day art project at school. Even my Chanel bag couldn't have made that necklace look more fashionable! But it was also the very first gift my dad had ever given me that was just from him. He had put time and thought into it, and that meant everything to me.

By accepting that necklace from my dad, I forgave him. While healing our relationship and my own PTSD would be a never-ending process, I accepted him then and there, flaws and all, and began to see the beauty buried within.

I still have this necklace tucked away in my jewelry box among many more expensive things. It is one of my most cherished pieces.

Before heading back to Chicago, my mom, dad, and I drove home to the farm. Though only a month had passed since my last visit for the intervention, so much had changed. While the one helicopter on the Lang farm had thrown me off before, there were now huge oil rigs everywhere. It was like a scene from a movie. Slowly but surely, checks had begun to arrive from the natural gas wells. They paid for my dad's rehab, they paid off our debts, and they would pay for my next two years of college. Undiscovered, untouched oil below the surface of the Lang farm saved my family and the legacy of our family farm from bankruptcy.

The next morning, I was packing up to go back to college. I shook the contents of my Chanel bag onto my bed. There it all was: my wallet, my DePaul University student ID, a few crumpled dollar bills, Carmex lip balm, loose receipts, and the blue beaded necklace that my dad had made me. I tossed the receipts and cleaned up my wallet. Just as I was about to toss the necklace back inside, I hesitated.

I thought about the past few years of suffering my entire family had been through, how far my dad had come, and how after all those years of misfortune, there was oil sitting just below the surface of the Lang farm. I wondered if within all of us there was a treasure that was waiting to be discovered, too. Maybe if I dug deep enough, I could actually become the type of woman that I thought was worthy of carrying a Chanel bag. Deep down, I knew that in order to do so, I'd have to take a hard look at what holes in my heart that Chanel bag was trying to fill.

I pulled the necklace over my head and left for the airport.

4

Trial and Error

DURING MY SENIOR YEAR OF COLLEGE, I FOCUSED all my anxious energy into getting my first job, setting my sights on a very big fish—*The Oprah Winfrey Show*. When I was growing up, my mother, her two sisters, and my grandmother Meme were obsessed with Oprah. They loved celebrity culture in general, and they worshipped few celebs as much as they looked up to and adored Ms. Winfrey. My mom in particular subscribed to anything and everything that Oprah suggested or touched. And, of course, in the Chicago area specifically, there was no bigger name than Oprah.

Early in the academic year, I got an interview for an internship in the production department of *The Oprah*

Winfrey Show. I prepared meticulously for that meeting and showed up looking the part in a black Theory suit that I'd dropped a pretty penny on at Celeste's. Like my Chanel bag, I saw that suit as a tool to help me tell the world who I was. While the bag evoked a confident, carefree spirit, to me that suit communicated power. When I pictured a powerful woman, I always imagined someone in a sharp designer suit. Wearing that suit, I believed I could own the room and get anything I wanted.

I held on to this belief even after I failed to get the job. If anything, the rejection solidified my determination to find another way in. My childhood and teen years had trained me well to single-mindedly pursue a goal until I achieved it, whether that was winning a swim meet, a beauty pageant, or a job. In high school, I swam for five hours before and after school to train for competitions. Even before that, I endured three years of pageant training, where I learned how to present myself as a proper beauty queen. I spent countless hours both in class and at home in front of the mirror perfecting my posture, crossing my legs at the ankles, and smiling in a way that looked natural but revealed nothing, not even my teeth.

I learned that I could get anything if I wanted it badly enough, and now I decided that I was going to work for Oprah no matter what. I reached out to my contact in HR relentlessly. She was French, and in my interview I had tried to show off by speaking the little French I had learned in high school and college, and to connect by telling her how I'd always dreamed of visiting Paris. Every month, I sent her an email saying Bonjour and reminding her that I'd be thrilled to take any opportunity that might become available. Finally, she offered me an internship in Oprah's public relations department. This is the same approach I took years later when reaching out to brands. Finding points of connection and building relationships are the best ways I've found to open any door.

That year, Shannon and I had branched off from our other roommates to get our own place. We settled on a classic brownstone with a tiny back patio and decorated it with vintage pieces we scored at local flea markets. My favorite piece was an antique television set that we had gutted out and turned into a fish tank to display in the living room. Shannon was in class when I got the call about my job at Oprah, so there was no one home to laugh at me as I jumped up and down on my flimsy Ikea bed screaming, "I got it!"

I was excited about the job, but I also felt a huge sense of accomplishment for having met such an enormous challenge. I know it sounds awful, but mostly I was excited about how working for Oprah would look on my résumé and how proud everyone would be of me back home. Looking back, I realize how superficial this was. I didn't even think about whether or not the job would bring me any sense of fulfillment. I was too focused on what other people thought of me, my self-esteem wrapped up in the perception of others. I wanted word to spread around my family and among my old high school friends that I was doing well and rocking the new life I had carved out for myself in Chicago.

I was just an intern, but I wanted to be taken seriously,

so I focused on presenting myself at work as professionally as possible. Besides my clothes, when I'd first moved to Chicago, the two things that people always noticed about me were my Southern accent and my blond hair. I stuck out in a sea of brunettes, and with my ADHD, I worried that I came off as a stereotypical ditzy blonde. It was also the first time I even realized that I had a Texas twang. Over beers at McGee's, our favorite local watering hole, my classmates and sorority sisters cracked up every time I said, "Y'all."

"That's so adorable," they laughed. "Say it again!" But I didn't want to be adorable. I wanted to fit in and come across as an adult, and to me, that meant losing my accent and having brown hair. I signed up for dialect courses, and right before starting the internship, I made the horrible decision to cut my hair short with bangs and dye it brown. I wish I could go back to that hairdresser and ask, "Why did you let me do that?" I may have looked grown-up on my first day of work in my Theory suit with my new haircut, but it definitely wasn't the most flattering look on me!

As the PR intern, my job was to put together a press kit each day that included every single mention of Oprah in the media. And let me tell you, there were a lot of them. After hand-delivering a copy of the press kit to everyone on the staff, I had to file each clipping by subject (from Oprah for President to Oprah and Gayle) in a never-ending hallway filled with hundreds of filing cabinets.

On my first day of work, I was bending down awkwardly in my suit to file something in the Book Club cabinet when a woman approached, walking toward me from the direction of Oprah's personal gym. The floor of that hallway was made of concrete, and it had a certain garage-like smell and feel. As I stood up, I smoothed my skirt and turned to greet the woman, who was wearing gym clothes with messy hair and no makeup.

It wasn't until after she'd already passed me with a quick "Good morning" that I even realized the woman who was standing inches away from me was, in fact, the one and only Oprah. She looked completely different from the glossy image of Ms. Winfrey that was imprinted on my mind. On TV, Oprah was larger than life, glowing, her presence nearly mythical. In person, off camera, she looked…normal. Human.

My whole life, I had believed that perfection was a real thing that actually existed in this world. Oprah had it. Mischa Barton's character on *The O.C.* had it. And if I tried hard enough and wore the right things and presented myself in just the right way, I could have it, too.

Now I saw that there was more to this simple equation than I had previously considered. Behind the filter of hair and makeup and wardrobe and celebrity, Oprah and the guests on her show weren't perfect, after all. They sweat after working out, too. Their hair got messy, too. My first glimpse of this made me want to keep peeling back those layers and dig deeper to see what was really hiding underneath their professionally constructed facades. If there were flaws anything like the ones I had under there, maybe that meant I could relax the standards I'd set for myself.

As soon as I started working for Oprah, my family started talking about coming to see a taping of the show.

My mom was already in Chicago, and after months of planning, her two sisters, Meme, and a bunch of my cousins all flew out to visit. It was a big deal. They bought new outfits, went out and got their hair done, and showed up at *The Oprah Winfrey Show* looking like they were ready for a visit with an actual queen.

I wasn't even sure if my family would have a chance to meet Oprah, but after the taping, we were hanging out in the cafeteria when Oprah came in to say hello and take a few pictures with us. When she walked in, I thought Meme was going to die of a heart attack on the spot. But she recovered quickly, immediately took over, and started directing Oprah to pose with each of us one at a time and then with the entire group.

I was cringing inside, but Oprah was kind and incredibly patient. I realize now that this was her gift to me for working as an intern. It was a pretty damn good gift that still hangs in my Meme's house today.

My family and I spent that entire weekend touring around Chicago, and I was excited to show off and play tour guide. They were so impressed with my life in the big city. Meanwhile, I absorbed their pride and awe with a certain amount of satisfaction, like a kid getting a gold star.

This was the same feeling I had every day when I got up and got ready to go to work. I always dressed up for work no matter how impractical it was, refusing to wear jeans even on casual Fridays. In my mind, I wasn't just dressing the part—I was living it. And the fact that this didn't translate into true feelings of contentment or fulfillment left me a bit confused and even ashamed. I asked myself,

Who wouldn't want to be wearing this suit to go work at The Oprah Winfrey Show? *Who wouldn't want a chance to talk to Oprah Winfrey herself every day? I even get to pet her dogs in her office! What is wrong with me?* Everyone around me thought it was amazing, but the truth was that their approval made me happier than the actual job.

It's not that I expected my day-to-day tasks to be fulfilling. I was only an intern and expected to spend most of my day either fetching coffee or filing press clippings. But I knew deep down that something else was missing, and I felt like something was wrong with me for not being satisfied with the incredible opportunity to work on *The Oprah Winfrey Show*. When I looked at the head publicist, my boss and mentor, I just couldn't see my life's work in her role one day. I felt so separate from it. It was almost like I was watching a movie about my life and my internship, but I wasn't actually in the movie.

However, I quickly became more interested in the show's production itself than I was in public relations. Whenever I had a free minute, I tried to sneak backstage or get a glimpse into the director's booth. This was where the magic happened. The executive producers, directors of photography, and hair and makeup and wardrobe stylists were the puppeteers to the carefully constructed and calculated empire that was *The Oprah Winfrey Show*. Did Oprah have an aura surrounding her? Absolutely. But the show itself ran successfully not only because of the talented Ms. Winfrey, but also because of the people who were behind the curtain. I wanted to be the one pulling the strings.

In the PR department, it was both eye-opening and disheartening to see how deceptive the media was. Every day, I filed article after article claiming that Oprah was running for president or getting married or recovering from a drinking binge, and I knew that none of it was true. I was learning that the lens I'd seen the world through my entire life was skewed. And part of me wanted to keep believing what I read in *Us Weekly*, where life was filtered and perfect-looking, just like I wanted to believe that I could dye my hair and put on a suit and change the lens through which the world saw me.

In my power suit, I was trying to fake it till I made it, but I was still just a lowly intern. My blond roots grew back each month, and my twang came out every time I had a couple of beers. Underneath it all, I was still that farm girl in bare feet and pigtails. I was still just me.

Turns out, I felt similarly after the first few times I wore my Chanel bag. I loved wearing it, but it also made me feel like a bit of an impostor. It wasn't enough to simply own the bag; I wanted to be the kind of person who I imagined would own that bag. Somehow, buying it hadn't transformed me into a self-assured, confident young woman the way I had expected it to. It hadn't transformed me at all, because no amount of labels and looks and likes can do that. Real transformation has to come from inside.

My mom and I both graduated from DePaul in the summer of 2006, her with a master's degree in music education and me with a bachelor's in communications. As a graduation gift, my mom gave me a silver David Yurman bracelet, which was one of the first nice pieces of jewelry I owned. That bracelet joined an elite group of trophy items in my wardrobe: my Chanel bag, the Theory suit, and a pair of Tory Burch flats that I'd saved up for and bought at Celeste's when they went on sale. When I wore them together, these items made my clothes from Target and Old Navy look a lot shinier. And anytime I had saved enough money, I added to this small but growing collection.

After graduation, my mom moved to Dallas to pursue her PhD, and I stayed in Chicago and got a job as a fashion writer at *StyleChicago*, a lifestyle website. I loved working there and getting more involved in fashion, but mostly I enjoyed the feeling of being an adult. My group of friends was scattering as they got new jobs and developed serious relationships, and I moved by myself into a condo in downtown Chicago.

I felt like Carrie Bradshaw, living alone in a big city, writing about life and fashion, and getting all dressed up professionally each day. Cue the *Sex and the City* theme song. I'd have the Chicago *RedEye* tucked under my arm and a black Tory Burch tote bag clutched in my left hand as I boarded the L train to work. My outfits were starting to grow more daring as I took more risks: pairing print on print, wearing distressed denim with my Tory Burch flats, incorporating lace tanks, more color, and bolder accessories.

I ended up leaving my job at *StyleChicago* because my bosses kept pushing me to do more sales and marketing and less writing about fashion. I was still young and saw my career as a process of trial and error. I was finding out what I wanted by learning what I didn't want. Very few people are born knowing what they want to do. My current job didn't even exist at this time! I never saw leaving a job as a failure, because I learned something new about myself in every role. At Oprah, I learned that nothing is as it seems, and at *StyleChicago*, I learned about incorporating advertising into editorial work. Every time I tried a new job, I was narrowing down the field, and I enjoyed going through the muck to find out what really made me tick.

I wasn't sure what my next move would be. A college friend of mine had moved to California a few months before and told me that there were great opportunities in Los Angeles. I remembered how much I'd loved learning about the production side of *The Oprah Winfrey Show*, and the idea of escaping Chicago for the winter and finding a temporary production assistant gig in sunny LA sounded pretty good. So, I loaded up my little Audi once again with as many of my belongings as I could fit and drove out to Los Angeles. When I got there, it was warm and welcoming in the middle of February, and I didn't ever want to leave.

I started freelancing for small production companies, not really knowing if and when I would ever return to Chicago. But I needed a place to live, so I found a studio apartment in Hollywood that was empty except for a mattress on the floor. I went back and forth to Chicago a few times and moved more and more of my belongings out West, and before I knew it and without really planning it, I was living in Los Angeles.

Soon after my arrival, I decided to get a dog to keep me company. After searching for weeks in the *LA Times*, I finally found an affordable litter of English bulldog puppies. When the runt of the litter rounded the corner of the breeder's apartment, we locked eyes and I knew he was the one. He was tan with white spots and some darker spots around the edges, and had tiny white stripes that divided his brown eyes. I named him William. Growing up, we had all sorts of dogs, stray cats, ducks, and pigs, but William was the first pet that was all mine. And he loved me back unconditionally, despite my imperfections. My love for William was the beginning of many, many steps toward my healing.

I was still consumed with other people's perceptions of me, and I wanted to find a full-time job that would legitimize my spontaneous move, not to mention provide me with a steady paycheck. It seemed like everyone I'd grown up around was getting an engineering degree, teaching school, or having babies. I knew they would roll their eyes at me for moving out West and pursuing an unconventional career. And my confidence was so flimsy that one eye roll could crush it. So, I looked for a steady corporate job in the entertainment field.

E! was considered the best broadcast news network in LA, so I focused my search there. Much like I had done to get the job at Oprah and connect with brands later, I followed up with E! consistently until I got an interview for a role as the assistant on a new show called *The Daily 10*. In my Theory suit, I turned some heads at my interview. In famously casual LA, I looked like I was going to work at the stock market. The woman who interviewed me was wearing a white T-shirt with jeans and a black blazer. But I still got the job.

Going from state to state, there was a huge swing in how people dressed. Growing up, I learned how to adjust my look for different occasions. I wore polo shirts with long skirts to school, floral sundresses that hit below the knee to church, Express navy blue pants with collared tops to pageants, and Wranglers with Justin brand boots to 4-H competitions. Now I was learning to adapt my style to my geographical location. It had taken me a year to learn how to dress in Chicago, and in LA I had to relearn everything.

Luckily, aside from my Theory suit and the other pieces I wore to try to look the part, my own personal style, which I was slowly starting to develop, was a natural fit with the casual West Coast vibe. Fashionista Jacey loves to dress up, but at the end of the day, I'm a farm girl at heart. These two Jaceys are two sides of the same coin, and it's both sides together that make me whole. Being in a creative place like LA, where personal expression was valued over most things, gave me the freedom to start allowing those two sides to blend into each other in a way that felt authentic and true to me.

This evolution took place over a long period of time. On my first day of work at E!, I looked super preppy in J.Crew pants, a cardigan, and my David Yurman bracelet. Everyone around me was wearing jeans and T-shirts (that each probably cost more than my monthly rent, but whatever), and I stuck out like a sore thumb as I went around introducing myself to the team. Finally, I approached the supervising producer, Stephanie, who was wearing the same David Yurman bracelet as me. More important, her

dry humor and desk proximity made her one of my closest confidantes at work.

My friendship with Stephanie was the first sign that I
might actually fit in at E!, but I had no idea what an important role my colleagues there would end up playing
in my life. Becoming friends with them felt like joining
my sorority all over again. We all went out for lunch and
drinks and weekend getaways and always had a blast together. They accepted me—flaws, quirky fashion choices,
and all. There were days when I showed up to work wearing jeans and a wrinkled button-down, and my new friends
poked fun at me in a loving way, just as my girlfriends back
in Chicago had about my awful winter coat.

"You do you, girl," my coworkers joked. They were
completely unpretentious and raw, which made me feel
comfortable being more open with them in return. I was
speaking to both of my parents again regularly, and as my
dad remained sober day after day and week after week, I
started to breathe a little. In the warmth of LA, the parts
of me that I hadn't realized were frozen slowly but surely
began to thaw.

During the day, I spent as much time as possible watching the stylists work with the on-air talent. I had become
good friends with Ashley, the fashion segment producer,
and Catt, the host of the show, and my bosses knew they
could always find me hanging out either in Catt's dressing room, at Ashley's desk chatting about the latest issue
of Us Weekly, or in the wardrobe closet. This is where my
interest in fashion really blossomed.

The infamous Monica Rose was Catt's stylist at the time,

and she later moved on to dress the Kardashian empire. Monica taught me simple things like where your pants should hit your ankle when you're wearing flats versus when you're wearing heels, how to pin clothes to make them fit better, the art of the cuffed sleeve on a shirt, and how to pop a collar and tuck your hair into it. From her, I also learned that you should strap your strappy ankle heel straps on the loosest hole to make your ankles look slim and the magic of wardrobe tape to create a temporary hem.

Monica showed me how to organize a rolling rack for fittings, pack a garment bag for an on-location shoot, and how to compliment talent on their looks. Remember the store Build-A-Bear, where you got to pick out pieces one by one to build your own perfect stuffed animal? When talent needed a bit of a pep talk or styling help, we joked that we'd Build-A-Bear them by putting them together, one article of clothing at a time, all while telling them how amazing they looked and how they were going to crush the red carpet.

My biggest takeaway was to buy less, choose well, and be bold with my style.

Meanwhile, I kept adding to my collection of trophy items with a black Hermès cuff bracelet that was super trendy at the time and a white Helmut Lang blazer. I had fun mixing high- and low-end labels in expressive new ways. Being surrounded by people like Ashley, Catt, Monica, and the show's makeup artist, Lina, gave me the courage to really go for it. They treated me like a younger sister. When the show taped in Las Vegas, we all ended up sharing a hotel room, even though the network paid for us to each have our own room. They helped me get ready to go out, using all their knowledge to give me advice on my outfits and how to do my makeup. While Lina did Catt's makeup, she said, "See, Jace? This is how you should draw your brows in… Here, take this pencil home and use it."

Thanks to these ladies and my burgeoning confidence, within my first year in LA, I went from wearing my Theory suit to work to wearing the blazer from the suit with distressed jeans, a T-shirt, my Chanel bag, and flats. I hit up Forever 21 about once a week to score a trendy new piece to throw into the mix of my wardrobe. I taped up a vision board inside my closet, and every time I got dressed, I mentally transported myself to the wardrobe closet at E! and imagined that I was Monica dressing the talent. This gave me more confidence to flip my collar or roll my sleeve, and with that confidence came bolder sartorial choices.

The combination of high- and low-end pieces that I favored was a new type of look at the time, and it intrigued Stephanie, who often asked how I put my outfits together.

"That's a Forever 21 top," she noticed, "and you're wearing it with that Yurman bracelet and a Chanel bag—how did you know to do that?" Or "I can't believe you got that dress at Target! How did you know to put a button-up blouse underneath?" I just shrugged. It wasn't something that anyone had taught me. It was just how I liked to dress.

One day, as I was messaging Stephanie about a new blazer I was buying from Forever 21, she messaged me back and said, You should start a blog!

So, I did.

Actually, I don't know that I would have even called it a

blog at that point, but I started a website called *JaceyLenae*. Lenae is my middle name, after my mom's best friend from college. On the site, I posted links of things I was thinking about buying and what I was wearing. There were no photos of me or text beyond a simple list of each item.

At the time, there were no "influencers," there was no "blogging industry," and the only people I considered fashion bloggers were *Fashion Toast* and *Who What Wear*. I really didn't give the website much thought. I enjoyed dabbling with it when I was bored, but I never had any inkling whatsoever that it would become anything more than a simple tool to share my outfits with a few friends.

One night shortly after I started the blog, Catt was out on a first date and I was in bed watching *American Idol* when she called me.

"You need to come and meet me," she said. "I can't tell if this guy is into me."

"I'm staying in tonight," I told her. "Have fun! I'm sure he's into you."

"Please," she begged me. "Just one drink. Please!"

I sighed. "Okay," I relented. "One drink. You owe me."

I showed up to Bar Marmont twenty minutes later in a black lace tank, skinny jeans, and strappy heels. As always, I had my white blazer draped over my shoulders. By the time I found Catt, she and her date were making out in a shiny red booth. "Pretty sure he's into you," I said once they came up for air and I had a chance to pull her aside. "I'm gonna go."

"No, no, you have to stay," Catt said. "Burke invited his friend Grant."

Great. I rolled my eyes. Now this was going to be a whole thing. I sat down and ordered a drink, feeling grumpy about the situation. I lamented that I hadn't listened to my gut and stayed in bed.

Then Grant walked in.

I wish I could tell you that it was love at first sight, or that I knew in that moment that we were meant to be together. Nah. He was cute, though, and he had a quiet confidence that put me at ease right away. More than anything, we hit it off as friends, joking around and laughing together as Catt and her date continued making out across the table from us. Grant had grown up in LA and was a real-estate developer with his own small business and a quirky sense of humor. Later that week, the four of us went out again. We had fun, but I wasn't looking for anything serious, and it didn't seem like Grant was, either.

In college, I always had boyfriends who made me feel insecure and needy, thanks to the drama I sowed in these relationships and my way of choosing guys who could best push my buttons. I didn't realize then that I was following the patterns that had been modeled to me by my parents. Mainly, I pushed my boyfriends away to test how much they loved me, a classic move by someone who doesn't truly believe they deserve love. I was afraid that if I fully gave someone my heart, they would leave me and I would be shattered.

About a week after I met Grant was my twenty-fifth birthday, and I threw myself a big "quarter-life party" at the Viceroy in Santa Monica. I was feeling good about life and was excited to have an excuse to celebrate. My dad was still sober, we'd been able to pay off our family debts, and although finances were still a struggle for me, I was earning a steady salary and fully enjoying my life in LA. It felt like winter was finally over and the thaw had fully set in. I invited Grant to the party, and I invited a couple of other guys I had gone on casual dates with, too. My friends teased me that it was like watching an episode of *The Bachelor.* Who was going to get the final rose? I told them I was having fun and wasn't taking any of it too seriously.

I went to Kitson, a very popular boutique on Robertson Avenue where all the celebrities were shopping during that time, and splurged on an expensive silk blue cocktail dress with white spaghetti straps and a flower at the top. Lina came over early and did my makeup and hair for the party, which made the whole event feel that much more special.

The party itself was fun and chaotic, and my attention was pulled in a million different directions all night long. I loved it. At one point, I noticed Grant walk in with a couple of friends. He was wearing a navy blue James Perse cardigan over a white T-shirt with fitted jeans and brown boots. He had a string hanging around his neck that looked like something he'd acquired on a spiritual retreat.

The hours flew by, and Grant and I didn't really have a chance to talk. It felt like I blinked, and suddenly it was late and the bar was empty. I was gathering my things when I looked over, and there in the corner was Grant. He wasn't trying to smother me or vie for my attention. He was just sitting there, waiting for me as if we had all the time in the world.

I went over to Grant with my drink, and we ended up talking for hours and laughing like old friends. It was just us two, cozied up in a tiny corner of a villa by the pool. Then, suddenly, he slowly leaned over and kissed me, and we didn't feel like friends at all.

From that night on, Grant and I were inseparable. But it was a slow burn between us. At our core, we were friends who loved and appreciated each other. There were no extreme highs and lows like I was used to. No drama. No insecurity. No doubt. No fighting. Just safety and security and friendship and love. I had learned what I didn't want, and this, finally, was exactly what I wanted. And needed.

I felt so comfortable in my own skin in my relationship with Grant. He had no pretense. He was genuine, and interesting, and completely different from anyone I'd ever dated. The first time we went out dancing, his friend Amos was DJ'ing at The Mandrake, a bar on La Cienega. At first, I was confused. He was playing old-fashioned stuff my parents listened to! And there was Grant, in a cardigan, dancing like a grandpa. It was my first time seeing that it was actually cool to just be yourself and let your freak flag fly.

There is a popular saying that goes something like, *You have to love yourself before anyone else can love you.* But that isn't true. Grant loved me for many years before I learned to love myself. With Grant, I could be everything that I was, and somehow, by some miracle, he still loved me. I had spent my whole life trying and trying and trying to fit in and be perfect, and I finally felt perfect just being me.

Even though Grant claimed to be allergic to dogs, after we'd been dating for a year, William and I moved in with him. A few months later, we talked ourselves into getting another English bulldog as a sister to William. We named her Polly, after the first movie we had ever seen together, *Along Came Polly*. Soon after, on my twenty-seventh birthday, Grant proposed in the kitchen as William and Polly shuffled at our feet. We spent the weekend celebrating our engagement at Chateau Marmont, where it had all begun.

After a year-and-a-half-long engagement, I took myself wedding dress shopping, alone. Yes, alone. I wanted to select something on my own terms without being swayed by anyone else's opinion. After hitting up Monique Lhuillier, Carolina Herrera, Oscar de la Renta, and Vera Wang, I kept going back to one dress from Vera Wang that was stuck in my mind.

Vera Wang wasn't a household name in South Texas, so it felt like I was choosing a big-city designer instead of a dress that was fit for a frilly Texas damsel. It was strapless with a lace detailed overlay and wild tulle at the bottom. I styled it with a black sash around my waist, which felt very edgy at the time, along with black Christian Louboutin satin pumps. When my mom came to my first fitting and she cried, I hoped that meant it was good.

Grant and I felt like it was us against the world, and this was reflected in our quirky wedding choices. We loved the idea of an urban wedding, and for our reception we chose a renovated old auto warehouse called the SmogShoppe. We rented vintage furniture and hired a bluegrass band to play during the cocktail hour. My mom and grandmother didn't love having the word *smog* on our wedding invitation or the fact that we chose to serve chicken and waffles and wrap our invitations in handkerchiefs. But it all felt very "us," very "Jacey and Grant."

William was our ring bearer, and Polly was our flower girl. Just after they walked down the aisle, I stood in the back adjusting the black sash on my dress. My dad approached me to take the walk that every girl dreams about. Until then, I hadn't really considered that this moment would one day be a reality.

"You look beautiful," my dad said. "I'm so proud of you."

It was the first time in a very, very long time that I had heard those words, and I couldn't help but cry as he walked me down the aisle, away from my past and toward my future.

I could not have been more excited for or more naive about how difficult that future might be.

5

The Blog Is Born

THE SUN WAS JUST WAKING UP IN THAILAND AS I opened my eyes and stretched my entire body out along the king-sized bed. Outside of our hotel room, birds chirped furiously, eager to start their day. Over their din, I could hear Grant singing in the shower. I smiled to myself, feeling that rare and precious sense of total peace and contentment. It was day seven of our honeymoon, and we'd gotten up early to visit an elephant sanctuary. I was excited for the day's adventure, but instead of hopping out of bed, I reached lazily for my laptop, wanting to hold on to that peaceful feeling for just a few moments longer.

I opened up WordPress, the hosting site for my blog, and logged in to the back-end site, which showed me a list of stats—total visitors, page views, etc. I had been up-dating the site in real time with pictures from our honey-moon. The only people who checked it were my parents and Justin and maybe a close friend or two who wanted to see what Grant and I were up to while we were away. I wasn't much of a photographer, but I was having fun play-ing around with the new camera I'd bought myself for our trip. I was basically treating the blog like a personal Face-book page, just a way of keeping folks back home posted on our adventures.

The day before, we'd done a ton of sightseeing, includ-ing a visit to a temple in Chiang Mai. There were two adorable little girls who were maybe five or six years old playing outside in front of the temple. I was struck by their colorful dresses, matching purses with embroidered pandas on the front, and traditional beaded headpieces.

"May I take your picture?" I asked them, gesturing to the camera around my neck in case they couldn't under-stand me. The two girls nodded shyly and posed side by side with their hands in prayer as I fumbled with the cam-era.

"Just a couple more," I said, frustrated with myself as I remembered to increase the shutter speed. The sun was beating down on us and glinting off the shiny golden tem-ple in the background.

I'd posted that picture, along with some others I'd taken at the temple and the local bazaar, when we'd gotten back to the hotel that night. Lazily checking in now, I expected to see the same kind of statistics I was used to—four or five unique visitors, maybe thirty page views in all. Instead, I saw a number that made me bolt upright in bed.

"Grant!" I shouted as I heard the shower turn off. "You have to see this!"

Grant came into the room, toweling off his hair. "What happened?" One thing about Grant—he's calm. No matter what's going on around him, he remains steady, constant.

I spun my laptop around for him to see. "My site got over thirty-five hundred views," I told him in disbelief. Many of them, total strangers, had left comments about the temple and the girls and asking for more info about our trip.

"What the hell?" I murmured, scrolling through. "This is so crazy."

"Huh," Grant said, leaning forward to take a closer look. "What do you think happened?"

"I have no idea."

I turned my computer back to face me and started clicking around to try to figure it out. I was certain it was a glitch or maybe just a typo. The back-end page showed where visitors were clicking into the site from, and for the vast majority of them, it simply said WordPress. That made no sense. WordPress was the hosting service for my site. Why would visitors be funneling in from there? Finally, I clicked through to the WordPress website to look for clues.

It didn't take much digging. There was a Freshly Pressed section on the WordPress home page, where they featured select blog posts. I frequented that section when I was bored at work or looking for some inspiration. I had no idea why, but that day they had chosen to feature my post.

It was a magical day. A guide picked us up from the hotel before the sun had fully risen and brought us to the Patara Elephant Farm, where we learned all about different species of elephants and were each paired with our very own elephant for the day. Bean You, my elephant, was an amazing, majestic creature. We had a chance to bond as I fed, brushed, and cleaned her. Then Grant and I rode our elephants bareback for a long trek in and out of rivers, next to rice paddies, and into the heart of the Chiang Mai jungle. Finally, we arrived at a waterfall, where we ate a beautiful lunch off huge banana leaves as our elephants played next to us in the water. It was truly perfect.

All day, I was totally present and content in the moment, but my happiness about the blog post hovered right around the edges of my mind. And every so often, the idea that something good had happened poked into my consciousness. Thirty-five hundred views! I was so honored that my picture had been chosen and that I'd been able to share something beautiful with all those people who weren't there with us to see it in person.

Though it was by far the most luxurious trip I'd ever been on, Grant and I were still on a budget for our honeymoon. So, we stayed in more affordable hotels for the majority of our trip and then splurged on our last few nights in Bali and stayed at the Blvgari Hotel. We had our own little villa on top of a cliff with a private pool overlooking the ocean. It was incredible. Grant and I were lying out by the pool as I daydreamed about what I was going to do when we got back to LA.

Right before we left for our honeymoon, I had quit my

most recent job as an assistant to one of Hollywood's biggest producers, Brian Grazer at Imagine Entertainment. Quitting had been an agonizing decision. I had only been at the job for a few months after leaving E! I was not a quitter, and it pained me to think of myself that way, but the job, with its fifteen-hour days and the unhealthy levels of competition among the producer's multiple assistants, had gotten to me. I knew there was no way I would have been able to take off two weeks and enjoy my honeymoon if I'd stayed at that job. Plus, I had seen what was at the top of that ladder I was grinding my way up, and I didn't really want it. The top executives at Imagine all seemed so stressed, and there was deep unhappiness behind their eyes. So, it wasn't worth it to me to keep putting in so much blood, sweat, and literal tears.

"I'm just sick of working for other people," I told Grant now with my eyes closed as I angled my face toward the sun. "But what else can I do? I'm not going to start my own company. I'm not going back to Texas to farm alongside my dad." I laughed out loud at the thought.

"Can you imagine?"

We both smiled as Grant floated on his back in the pool just a few feet away from me. He looked thoughtful.

"You've been really into your blog," he said. "Do you think you could keep doing that? Maybe design sites for other people to make some cash?"

I looked at Grant. What he was saying sounded amazing, but I had never considered anything like that as an actual career option.

"I didn't go to school for that," I reminded him. "I'm

not a graphic designer or a coder. I've just been learning as I go. Why would anyone hire me?"

I was getting worked up, but Grant remained impassive, practical.

"I could name ten people I know in LA who probably need a new website right now," he said. "Start with them. Build a portfolio. Take some classes. I can float us for a bit financially if this is something you want to do."

I sat up on the lounger and started tapping both of my feet as I looked at Grant, a smile forming on my lips. Until then, I had never allowed myself to imagine how it would feel to devote myself to something creative full-time, something that belonged to no one else but me. I had been so busy trying to build a résumé that would look impressive to other people. But as I'd gotten to know myself, I realized that those jobs that looked so good on paper weren't fulfilling for me. Maybe being true to myself didn't just mean a quirky wedding or an atypical honeymoon. It had to extend to all corners of my life, including the very center of what I did for work each day.

When we got home from the honeymoon, I didn't dip a toe in or get my feet wet or any other metaphor for starting something slowly. I dived in headfirst and devoted every ounce of my energy to the blog. For the first time, I was using my ADHD to my benefit. I was hyper-focused on something I felt passionate about, and it all just clicked. I realized that I didn't have to let my ADHD hold me back. Instead, I could use it to thrust myself forward.

The first thing I did was respond to every single comment I'd gotten on my honeymoon pics. The mostly women who'd visited the blog wanted to know more about what hotels we'd stayed at and other sites we'd visited. Some were even asking about my life back home.

I started emailing with many of these women, wanting to learn more about their own lives and the type of content they wanted. I learned that while they were super interested in travel, they had tons of questions about fashion. They wanted to know what I'd worn on my honeymoon and asked me what they should wear to various events and outings. It was amazing to me that these women looked at me as some sort of expert when I had started the blog just for fun. But this was an opportunity to use my own passion for clothes to turn it into something these women might find truly valuable.

I started posting more frequently and putting together content to meet my new followers' needs. One woman asked me what to wear on an upcoming fly-fishing trip, so I posted an entire outfit with links to buy each item. Another reader asked me for links to everything I was purchasing that month for my closet, and another wrote in asking for advice on what to wear to her engagement shoot.

I enrolled in coding classes so I could learn how to code HTML better. But I was mostly self-taught, googling and watching YouTube videos to learn how to do things as I was doing them. I was excited by Grant's idea of creating websites for other people and knew that I needed an example of my work to attract clients. So I offered to create a site for his sister, an aspiring singer, for free. She came over to our condo, and we drank wine while messing around with templates and various designs for hours.

It didn't feel like work at all, even after I started charging other friends and neighbors five hundred dollars per site and set up my own company, Jolly Bulldog, in honor of William and Polly. I put so much work into each site that if you broke that rate down hourly, it would have been hilariously low. But it still felt like stealing to get paid to do something I truly enjoyed.

When I wasn't designing sites for other people, I was working on my own blog, emailing with my followers, and researching other fashion and travel blogs so I could learn more. Blogs had been around for a long time, but the idea of anyone making their living from a blog was brand-new. There were very few people who had a blog as a career, and it sounded like a fantasy to me.

At this point, I was less concerned about making money from my own blog. I wanted to continue doing it as a creative passion and make ends meet by earning money off Jolly Bulldog. But I needed to level up.

We were still skating by and mostly living off Grant's income, and I hated it. I wanted to contribute more financially, and the idea of being able to do that while doing something I loved that didn't involve going to an office and working for someone else seemed too good to be true. But I was determined to figure out how to make it happen.

Everything I was doing felt right in a way it never had before, and I would've done anything to hold on to that feeling. For the first time in my life, I didn't need external validation because I was truly fulfilled by my work. Working in our living room, wearing jeans and a tank with my bare feet on the coffee table, I felt more powerful than I ever had in my Theory suit.

Through my research, I discovered that there were blogging conferences where I could learn more about the industry. The Alt (short for Altitude) Summit in Utah seemed like the most important one, and I saved up over several months to buy a ticket. This was the first real investment I made in my blog, and it was more than worth it.

Over the weekend-long conference, I learned about web design, posting cadence, editorial calendars, and branding. I felt completely naive—this was all new to me—and yet I was a total sponge, soaking so much in that it felt like it was bursting out of my skin. And hanging out with the other bloggers over coffee and drinks before and after the panels and talks was just as educational. I learned about all the hard work they were doing behind the scenes to create content, design their blogs, and brand themselves. All of these confident, successful, put-together women were basically stylish computer programmers. They motivated me to put in any amount of work necessary to achieve success and that same level of confidence.

When I got home, I couldn't wait to tell Grant all about the conference. I had barely wheeled my suitcase past the front door before I was filling him in on every detail of whom I'd met and what I'd learned.

"Babe, I need a name!" I shouted to him as he went into the kitchen to pour us some wine. He poked his head back into the living room with a quizzical expression on his face. "For the blog," I laughed. I was still just calling it *JaceyLenae*. "All the other girls have cute names like *The*

Blonde Salad or *Cupcakes and Cashmere*. I need something witty like that."

"Hmm…" Grant ran a hand through my hair and took a sip of his wine. "The Blonde Burrito?"

"Grant! No!" I giggled, feeling like a bottle of champagne that someone had shaken up.

"Well, what do you want it to be like?" he asked me. "When they hear the blog's name, how do you want people to feel?"

I took a deep breath to settle myself and thought about it.

"The women who read my blog are cool. I want them to feel like…" I stared out the window, trying to find the right words. "Like they're in control of their lives. Like they can dress however they want and be whoever they want. Basically, the opposite of that lost little girl I used to be who always felt like a damsel in distress."

"So, instead of a damsel in distress, how about…Damsel in Dior?"

I looked at Grant. "I love that," I said quietly, leaning in for a kiss. "And I love you!"

My bags went unpacked (a huge deal for me) as I immediately dug into rebranding my blog as *Damsel in Dior*, using everything I'd learned at Alt Summit. The first thing I did was create an editorial calendar and commit to sticking with it for two months to see how my following grew in that time. My schedule was: Corporate Mondays (featuring a work-appropriate outfit), Beauty Tuesdays (hair and/or makeup), What I Want Wednesdays (a shopping post), Champagne Thursdays (hosting tips, inspired by

my Chicago days), and Fun Night Friday (with a fun outfit for going out).

In between, I experimented. I never sought out to be just
a fashion blog or a travel blog. Life is all-encompassing, and
the blog was, too. But my readers were naturally more interested in some things than others, and I continually tweaked
my content to meet their needs.

It was fascinating to me to see what my readers responded
to and what they didn't. One week, I posted about a great
fish taco recipe I'd tried, and it was met with crickets on
the blog. But just a week later, I posted a margarita recipe
and it got a huge response. It wasn't random. I found that
certain content received more clicks and comments on
specific days of the week. For example, drink recipes got
more clicks on Thursdays, while fitness posts were more
popular on Mondays.

After two months, my stats were more consistent and
growing steadily, so I decided to stick with the editorial
calendar I had created. The whole time, I was engaging
with readers very intimately, one-on-one. They told me
about their upcoming vacations, and I put together entire packing lists for them and posted them on the blog. I
showed them how to style the same items from those lists
in different ways, because this was real life and, of course,
they would wear the same clothing multiple times.

It was never about how many followers I did or didn't
have. There was no Instagram, or social media, or temp-
tation to keep score. It was just me and my readers, and
I appreciated and valued every single one of them. They
sent me photos of themselves wearing the outfits we had

put together, videos of their engagements, and long-form stories about how they, too, always felt misunderstood or like a damsel in distress. By focusing on this, I continued to make the blog about my readers instead of about me and my personal life.

This all changed a few months after Grant and I got back from our honeymoon. I had submitted our wedding photos to *Style Me Pretty*, a wedding site that I had been obsessed with when we were planning our wedding. After they chose our photos to be highlighted, it brought a huge number of new readers to my blog. It was so exciting, but these readers wanted to know all about me and even Grant. They asked for more details about the wedding, the honeymoon, and our lives in LA.

I was determined to create the content that my followers wanted, and what they wanted could not have been clearer. When I posted a picture of myself and what I was wearing, I got triple the views and triple the comments of any other post. This gave me pause. Since meeting Grant and then devoting myself to the blog, I had been feeling more authentically like myself than I had, well, ever. For once, my life wasn't about pleasing other people, either through impressive titles and accomplishments or picture-perfect looks. I was getting a taste of what it was like to be respected for my other talents, not just for what I looked like or what I wore, and I wanted to keep going in this direction.

I was worried that posting pictures of myself and what I was wearing would awaken the people-pleasing beast and put too much of an emphasis on the Jacey that loved fashion and dressing up. As I finally began to feel complete, I was determined not to let Farm Girl Jacey slip away while making her fashionable counterpart look perfect on the blog. The real me was somewhere in between the farm girl and the fashionista.

Putting myself out there for the world to see was terrifying, not least of all because I worried about what my family back home would think. So, yeah, I guess that whole people-pleasing thing was still in effect. My family obviously didn't understand what I was doing. The blogging industry was so new that few people did. But as much as I wanted to be true to myself, every time I posted about getting drunk over the weekend or laughing so hard that I peed my pants, I cringed internally, wondering what my mother and Meme would think.

It was around this time that I finally joined Instagram, and even then only after my friends basically browbeat me into it. I admit that I was late to the Instagram party, especially compared to my fellow bloggers. This was partially because I was so focused on the blog itself, but also because I knew that with its focus on the visual, it is inherently superficial. I knew it might make me feel insecure and competitive about how I looked.

The compromise I made with myself was to give my readers more of what they wanted and start sharing images on Instagram, but to retain my raw and honest touch in my writing. In many ways, the writing I did for the blog scratched the same itch as the stories I wrote about my dad in college. It provided an outlet where I could share what was really going on behind the glossy, curated pictures I posted on my feed.

I was having a blast writing and creating, but I wasn't making money from the blog until a company called rewardStyle reached out to me about six months after the honeymoon. They were a brand-new affiliate network that said they would provide me with links to the items I was already posting about. When my readers clicked on those links and purchased items, I would receive a small percentage of the sale. The idea that this would actually lead to anything seemed like a long shot, but I just thought, *Why not?*

I was honestly shocked to see that once I got into the flow of it, those small commissions really started to add up. It was fascinating to see what was selling and what wasn't and to try to figure out how to adjust my content to increase sales. If someone bought a blazer through my link, I'd buy the same blazer, post about different ways of styling it, and watch sales of that blazer triple. It was the same type of work I had enjoyed doing at Celeste's, but in a different format and on a larger scale.

After Grant was in bed and the stars were out, I spent hours tracking the activity of my readers on the site through Google Analytics and editing my content based on their behavior. If they were clicking out of the site from a certain page, I'd add new content to keep them there or a link to another page on the site so they wouldn't exit out. It was like solving an endless puzzle, and it was so satisfying to watch readers' behavior change in real time based on these tweaks.

No one told me what to do or how to do it. I was very much making it up as I went along, drawing inspiration from my readers and fellow bloggers. I simply woke up and geeked out every day, experimenting and obsessing over the results.

One morning, over coffee, I stared at a fellow blogger's post that was getting a huge response, wondering how she got the picture of herself in the street. I ran to the closet and put together an outfit. I dressed in a white tank that had gold beads on it with a black cropped blazer, black cuffed pants, and heeled oxford lace-ups. I ran outside just as Grant was getting into his car.

"Babe, do you have a second?" I asked. "I need your help with a pic."

"Okay, real quick," he said, following me out to the street as I handed him my camera. "I've gotta meet the electrical crew over in Venice."

I checked for traffic and ran across the street, feeling quite silly as I posed with one hand in my pocket and my other arm awkwardly hanging by my hips, looking down and away from the camera so my eyes weren't visible. To this day, I always wear sunglasses or try to find another creative way of hiding my eyes in pictures. It's my way of keeping something to myself.

Grant snapped a few pictures and then held the camera out for me to see. I ran back to him as quickly as I could in my heels.

"Oh, I didn't notice that pole there. That looks weird," I mumbled as I scrolled through. "Can you take one more just a few feet down?"

"Babe, I gotta go," Grant said, bending forward to kiss me. "Sorry."

I sighed and ran back inside, got out my tripod, and set

it up in the middle of our parking garage so no one would see me. By the time I got back in position, I was sweating and my hair was starting to frizz. Just then, a car started coming down the ramp. I stared at my expensive tripod and camera just a few feet away. I really didn't want anyone to see me, the narcissistic neighbor, taking pictures of herself in the parking garage.

Thinking fast, I kicked off my heels, ran to grab the tripod, and hid behind the trash bins while our neighbor made his way upstairs. By the time I caught my breath, got the tripod set up again, and finally got the shot I wanted, I was dripping with sweat, my makeup had all run off, and I was exhausted. I took a quick shower, changed into jeans, a white T-shirt, and flip-flops, fell onto the couch, and got back to work. Whew.

The whole time, I was designing sites for other people through Jolly Bulldog. I saw web development as my main job and the blog as a side hustle. But after about a year of working from seven every morning until late at night on both, I had designed about thirty websites, but the balance had shifted. Now I was earning more money from the blog than I was as a web designer.

I was just beginning to see the blog's full potential and wanted to devote more time and energy to it, but I also had clients depending on me. And the truth is I was scared to let go of the legitimate-sounding title of web developer and become a full-time blogger. It felt like a huge risk. Full-Time Blogger was not a title I had ever seen on an aptitude test or a list of viable career options. Would everyone think I was being silly and irresponsible? On top of that, what if I couldn't make it work? What if all my hard work amounted to nothing and I was left with a giant hole in my résumé? What if I failed?

I was scared, but I also couldn't deny where my heart and energy and passion were, and those rewardStyle checks didn't lie, either. I knew that if I took all the time, effort, and energy that I was still pouring into Jolly Bulldog and redirected it toward my blog, I would make double the amount from commissions. Looking at that number, I could justify taking the leap of faith. It was a tough decision, but I finally stopped taking on clients, shut down Jolly Bulldog, and devoted myself completely to *Damsel in Dior*.

One of the first things I did was sit down on one of the three tan leather stools at our kitchen island. I took out a fresh Moleskine journal and my favorite pen that I had snagged from The Peninsula in Beverly Hills and wrote out a professional bucket list. At the time, the items on my list felt truly unachievable: to be featured in *Vogue* and *Architectural Digest*, to be photographed by Bill Cunningham, to design a capsule collection, to be named one of the Top 25 Publishers by rewardStyle, to create my own cotton clothing line, to go backstage at Dior, and to earn a million dollars in a year. I was just a Texas girl with a WordPress account, a love of fashion, and lofty goals. How would I ever achieve them?

To start inching my way in the direction of my dreams, on a blank page I wrote out my expected income for the year, my number of followers, my conversion rate, my goals for the coming year, and my goals for the next quarter. The first time I did this, I had 37,963 followers on Instagram and about 8,306 daily readers checking my blog. I made the goal of hitting 100,000 followers on Instagram in the next year (I made it to 153,000) and 150,000 daily readers for the blog. I still write out these details in the exact same journal, and that original bucket list on the first page has never changed.

Fueled by equal parts passion and fear, I knew that if I was going to reach any of those goals, I had to take ownership and create more opportunities for myself. I started cold-emailing other bloggers who'd started at around the same time as me, asking if they wanted to collaborate. A group of us got together and tried on a new line of swimsuits from a designer I'd met, and we each posted about it. Things like this, that didn't pay, led to more clicks, more eyes on the blog, and more connections within the industry. Those other bloggers started inviting me to their events, where I'd meet more people, and this led to new collaborations, more invites, more networking, and more hustle.

I still didn't have a lot of money to spend on clothes to showcase on the blog, especially after shutting down Jolly Bulldog, so I had to get creative. I went to the J.Crew store at The Grove, a huge outdoor mall in Los Angeles, and bought a few hundred dollars' worth of clothes. Then I took them home, spent an entire day shooting myself in the different outfits, and returned everything. I did this multiple times.

One day, I walked into the store with a huge bundle of clothes to return. The salesperson, whom I'd seen many times before, cocked his head at me.

"Why don't you just do a pull?" he asked me.

I looked at him, confused. I had no idea what he was talking about, but I didn't want to seem like a total idiot. Plus, was I getting busted?

"Excuse me?" I asked, pretending I hadn't heard him.

"A pull," he said again as one by one he scanned in my returns. "I asked why you don't do a pull."

"Can you spell that?" I guess not seeming like an idiot was off the table.

He smiled and leaned forward, probably taking pity on me.

"All the film crews and stylists do pulls," he explained. "You borrow what you need, pay a ten percent restocking fee, keep whatever adds up to that ten percent, and return the rest."

I blinked at him. "So," I said, wanting to make sure I understood properly, "if I pulled two thousand dollars' worth of merchandise, I would pay two hundred dollars and keep two hundred's worth?"

"You got it," he told me. "You want to fill out the form?"

God bless that sales associate! This changed the game for me in terms of being able to create more and more content. I waited until I needed to buy new clothes anyway and did a huge pull. This gave me tons of content that I could spread out over the coming months. I didn't limit myself to J.Crew, either. Now that I knew this existed, I started walking into the stores I already shopped at and asked if I could do a pull.

I kept track of how much I sold of each brand and each

item through rewardStyle, and eventually I started reaching out to brands directly. I didn't have an in. I scoured the web the old-fashioned way to find out who did each brand's marketing. Then I emailed them, introducing myself, told them how much of their brand's merchandise I had sold on my blog, and asked for a gift card to continue to post about their brand.

I only posted about the brands and items I would have bought anyway, so there was never a conflict of interest. The only difference was that now I wasn't going into debt buying things to post about. This remained true after I slowly but surely worked my way up to asking brands to pay me to post.

But my first real paid gig as a blogger came from an unexpected source. My friend Isabelle was working at a lifestyle website called *PopSugar* that had partnered with Levi's, and she was encouraging them to work with me. It was perfect. I had grown up on a cotton farm and, of course, Levi's are made of cotton. I put together a pitch that included a trip to Texas for the Fourth of July to shoot the video. The people at Levi's loved it, and they sent Grant and me to Texas with a bunch of professional cameras and a shot list.

We had no idea what we were doing, but we had a blast shooting on the farm. I posed in my Levi's on a tractor and in the fields, and it felt like Grant and I were dating again as we laughed together and played around in the endless white expanse of cotton. Since he'd gotten sober, my dad and I had been slowly rebuilding our relationship, and I had reached the point of trusting him again. Even my mom had moved back in after completing her degree, and she and my dad were trying to make their relationship work. My mom's faith in my dad gave me hope, and watching him teach Grant how to drive a tractor and explain the entire process of how cotton is planted, grown, and sent out to factories made my heart feel full.

Shortly after returning to Los Angeles, we moved out of Grant's condo into a house we rented in West Hollywood. That house, and the life we shared in it, was everything I'd ever wanted. There was a little studio out back that I converted into my home office, so I finally had a space of my own to work in. When we weren't working—me on the blog and Grant on his real-estate development business—we were hosting parties and hanging out and having fun.

It felt like we were really building something, each of us individually and together as a couple. I was in love with Grant, and I was in love with my job. It was as if I was on a roller coaster going up, up, up, and then, for just a moment, it hung in midair.

6

The Cost of Perfection

IT WAS OBVIOUS TO ME EARLY ON THAT IF I WANTED to establish myself in the fashion industry, New York was the place to do it. That's where the majority of fashion houses, PR companies, and marketing reps in the industry were located, and I knew exactly no one at any of them. But I quickly set out to change that.

The first few times I traveled to New York, I really had no reason to be there. I spent hours online searching for email addresses of people who worked at different brands, magazines, and marketing and PR companies and cold-emailed them, simply saying that I was going to be in New York on a certain day and asking if they had time to meet for coffee. When I got back to LA, I always sent a personal note to each person for taking the time to meet. Sometimes I added a candle with a note saying, *Thanks for brightening up my trip to the city. Hope to catch you next time!*

These trips were an investment of time and money, but I immediately saw a return. Slowly but surely, I was building relationships in the industry, and the people I met with started expecting me to be in New York. Every time I visited, I took photos of whatever hotel I was staying in, often the Empire Hotel in Columbus Circle, geotagging the location and tagging the hotel. When the hotel left a comment saying, Thanks for staying with us! I immediately responded, offering additional photos I'd taken for them to use on their social media channels. This was how I slowly developed relationships with hotels to stay for a media rate and then later for a full trade (for free in exchange for posts).

Knowing that I was popping in and out of the city often, publicists and designers slowly started to invite me to events, and I began planning my trips around the biggest events that I was invited to each month. This helped me get content for the blog and more followers, more connections, and more invitations. It was a domino effect. Before I knew it, I was in New York twice every month. It felt like my home away from home, and I looked forward to seeing the flight attendants and hotel concierges, who knew me by name, almost as much as I looked forward to seeing my friends at home.

Back in LA, Grant was busy grinding, too. He was flipping houses and building development properties and had a lot of big projects in the pipeline. At first, he didn't question me when I said I had to go to New York for meetings, but when the lease came up on our expensive rental house, we started talking more seriously about the future.

We knew that eventually we both wanted to own our own home and start a family, and that would require planning. Real estate in Los Angeles is and was ridiculously expensive, so we agreed that the best move would be to take advantage of Grant's expertise and buy a house and flip it. We could save a ton of money by having Grant manage the renovation. But at that point, we didn't have enough saved to buy a modest house to flip. Most of Grant's income was going to our rent and expenses. I was starting to make decent money with the blog, but I was putting every penny that I earned back into the business.

"Maybe you should think about cutting back on your expenses," Grant told me one night as we sat side by side at the edge of the pool with our feet in the water. It was cool out, too cold to swim, but the chilly water felt good against my feet.

I turned my head to look at him, feeling my heartbeat quicken. "What do you mean?"

"Well, if we want to buy a house, we need to save up for the down payment," he said calmly. "We can cut back on some of our personal expenses, and we should each look at our business expenses. Are all the clothes and trips really necessary?"

I took a deep breath in an effort to stay calm but could feel my expression harden.

"I'm doing everything I can," I told him, immediately going into defensive mode. "I'm flying at the back of the plane. I'm pulling clothes. I'm doing trades with the hotels. Other than that, yes, it's necessary to strengthen and grow the business. Trust me. It's all going to work."

"Why are you getting so upset?" Grant's tone didn't change. "We don't have to fight." I looked down at my feet floating in front of me. The water was bracing. "I believe in you, Jace," he continued, "but it's simple math. If we don't start putting more into savings, we're not going to be able to buy a house. What do you want?"

I was torn. I did want a house and a family and all of the same things as Grant. I mean, eventually. And I had to admit that he knew a lot more about money and how the world worked than I did. I had zero experience with money, and in many ways I was still completely naive. I believed what Grant was saying and knew that, of course, he only wanted what was best for both of us. But in my heart, I was resistant and a bit resentful of the fact that he was asking me to cut back.

I was only twenty-eight years old, doing something I was good at, and earning a living while doing it. So, I asked myself, why was Grant telling me that I couldn't spend my own hard-earned money? It wasn't like I was being frivolous. I knew that I could keep getting a return if I invested in my business now, so it was hard to agree to put it toward the future instead. Plus, I liked the easy, carefree life we were living now and was happy to put the future off just a little bit longer.

What I didn't realize at the time was that I was doing the same thing I had done in the past—pushing people away before they could hurt or abandon me. On some level, I could feel that Grant and I weren't fully giving ourselves to each other. We were both holding something back. It was too scary to go all in or to voice my concerns. So, instead I kept moving forward while silently building resentment toward Grant and toward myself.

If I had to look back and pinpoint a moment when the first tiny fissure appeared in the foundation of our marriage, it was that conversation out by the pool. Nothing changed after that overnight. We didn't even really fight. In fact, we never really fought. We loved each other and wanted the same things. And yet it was easier for me to tell myself that Grant wasn't being supportive and to believe that he was trying to hold me back.

This was also when it started to bug me that I was traveling so much alone, even though no one was forcing me to take those trips, and I knew full well that Grant was busy working at home while I was gone. As the holiday season approached, I was back in New York pitching Banana Republic on a sponsored post. For a while, I had been meeting every month or so with my contact there, a sweet redhead named Robin. We really connected and genuinely liked each other. Ever since the Levi's gig, I had slowly started to work on pursuing more brand partnerships and sponsored posts. Banana seemed like a good place to start since Robin and I had such a strong relationship. Plus, I already shopped there and posted about their clothes.

Over lunch at the Gramercy Park Hotel, I shared my idea with Robin and casually mentioned that I had a deck to see if she was interested. Little did she know that I had already spent close to six hours of research, graphic design,

and Photoshop creating a pitch to shoot a video promoting
Banana Republic's holiday line, which included a nice va-
riety of cozy, dressy neutrals like white wool skirts, sparkly
scarves, and knit hats and gloves for gifting.

"I love this," said Robin. "Who do we need to work
with to negotiate your fee?"

"Just me," I said, closing down my laptop.

"Oh, great," she responded with a huge smile. "That
definitely makes our lives easier."

I knew that most bloggers who were getting sponsored
fees from brands were represented by management companies, but I was still flying solo and considered it an asset.
As I negotiated my own fees and managed every single aspect of my career, I got to know more and more people in
the industry, and they loved the fact that they didn't have
to go through a third party to work with me.

I was highly aware of the fact that at the end of the day,
I was just another blonde girl from Texas who was posting
about her life on social media. There was nothing truly
special about that. The only thing that set me apart was my
relationships, both with my readers and with the brands
I posted about. So that's where I put the vast majority of
my time and energy.

Sure enough, a contract for the Banana Republic deal
came through just as I arrived back at my hotel that night.
Smiling to myself, I scrolled through my recent calls and
let my finger hover over Grant's name. I wanted to share
the good news. He had come up with the concept for the
pitch that included shooting at an ice-skating rink where
Grant played in a hockey league. But I was suddenly re-

sentful of the fact that he wasn't there to share the good news with me in person. And it was convenient to believe that I was alone in that hotel room because Grant was the bad guy, not because of anything I had or hadn't done.

During that time in my marriage, it felt like we were going through the motions. Neither Grant nor I had ever been given a true model of what it meant to be in a strong, healthy, loving marriage, and we'd had no idea what we were really signing up for when we tied the knot. When we met, everything had seemed so perfect. First came love, then came marriage, then Jacey started a fashion blog and her relationship took a back seat.

Where was the raw, hot, passionate love from the movies where the guy flies to New York City to surprise his girl in the hotel room with rose petals on the bed? Of course, that's not what marriage is really like, but I was holding our relationship to that unrealistic standard because it was the only model I'd seen of relationships besides my parents', which I knew was unhealthy. When my marriage didn't live up to those expectations, it felt like something was wrong. This only exacerbated my own feelings of insecurity. What was wrong with our relationship? More to the point, what was wrong with me?

Over the next few weeks, I had a blast creating not one, but two holiday videos for Banana Republic, obsessing over every detail to make sure they were absolutely perfect. I always made it a point to under-promise and over-deliver. This led to more sponsored posts and partnerships and, ironically, a meeting with a management company that reached out about wanting to represent me.

I was willing to entertain the idea, but I remained unconvinced. Thanks to my strong relationships with the people at the brands I worked with, they told me that they were paying me at least as much per post as my fellow bloggers who had representation. Plus, I didn't have to hand over a 15 percent commission to a manager. Yet I knew there had to be some reason that so many of the biggest names in the blogging industry were working with this management company, so I figured I would hear them out.

After they reached out several times via email, I finally agreed to take a meeting with a big-league manager at DBA named Karina. I didn't want to look too overdressed, so I opted for an A-line black dress with tights and brown ankle booties. I draped a leather jacket over my shoulder and carried a Tory Burch bag. An hour later, the elevators opened to reveal five long rows of desks buried in gift baskets and shopping bags, where assistants typed away. Along the opposite wall were five large offices with glass windows, filled with talent agents with headsets on, making hand gestures to their assistants while typing away at their own computers. Jake, Karina's incredibly sweet assistant, gave me a short tour and then sat me in a small office with a bottle of Pellegrino.

I crossed my legs at the ankles, just as I'd been taught to do in my pageant days, as not one, but three managers were ushered into the office. For a minute, I felt important. Then I listened to the managers talk at me about so many things I already knew and had done on my own, and once again I questioned why I should sign the dotted line with an agency.

Suddenly, I felt the energy in the room shift. Some people sat up straighter. Others started fidgeting. I noticed that a few were looking over my shoulder. I turned my head so I could see through the glass wall of the conference room into the reception area. A very successful and famous blogger named Erika was walking in, wearing black skinny jeans, over-the-knee boots, and an off-the-shoulder white fuzzy sweater. She looked flawless.

"Well, Jacey, it has been so wonderful to meet you," Karina said, leaning forward as if she was about to stand up. "Our next meeting is here, but we're looking forward to continuing the conversation."

I looked at the huge clock on the wall over her head. I had only been there for fifteen minutes. As the rest of the team got up, shook my hand one by one, and filed out of the room, I sat there for a moment in shock. Had they really just cast me aside for someone more important? A huge wave of insecurity started rolling toward me. *Of course they did*, my inner voice told me. *You're just a stupid little farm girl. They can see right through you.*

I tried my best to push back against that voice. *Wait a minute*, I thought. *They were the ones who were pursuing me.* There would always be people out there with bigger names and more followers, but I had been succeeding so far on my own. I didn't need anyone's approval to keep doing exactly that.

As insecure as I often felt in my personal life, I was confident in my business. The facts were there in black and white: analytics, statistics, sales. Even my most doubtful self couldn't ignore those. It was one of the reasons why I poured so much of myself into work. It was the one area of my life where I felt truly confident—the one thing I felt like I could control.

I politely declined the management company's offer to represent me and kept pushing harder. The nature of blogging at this time was for everything to be presented as beautiful and perfect. I tried to hold on to my authenticity, but perfectionism was a powerful drug for me, and I was good at it. I obsessed over every detail of my pictures and my posts, wanting to prove to myself, to Grant, to the management company, and to the whole world that I was the real deal and that all the hard work and time I was putting into this blog was worth it.

I knew I was running the risk of missing out on bigger deals by not signing with the agency. A lot of ad agencies and companies like Amazon went straight to management companies to seed out their budgets to the bloggers, YouTubers, and influencers on their rosters. And yours truly was on no roster at all. The only way to keep up was to work harder than anyone else.

I had an assistant who worked for me part-time, mostly unboxing packages, creating my travel itineraries, and double-checking my blog for spelling errors. But as my business grew, so did my needs. When work started to slip and emails started to go missing, I knew it was time to hire someone to help me handle the business from head to toe.

A young woman named Haleigh had cold-emailed me looking for a job, which I found very impressive. As soon as I met Haleigh, I knew I could trust her with the role. She was only eight years younger than me and reminded me so much of myself. She was self-deprecating and seemed highly motivated to do good work and be successful.

Even with Haleigh's help, I stayed up until midnight most nights working, and I barely ate. I became so overly focused on the small details of a picture or my holiday gift guide that the slightest distraction, like the sound of a lawn mower outside my office, was completely unraveling. I went from hyper-focused and in the zone to feeling like I was in a war zone inside a tent with the walls shaking. The more distracted I got, the tighter I tried to hold on to control, and then I spiraled into anger and rage when I couldn't focus. I'm embarrassed to admit now that I had so little control of myself and screamed at the gardeners, "I'm trying to work!" As if they weren't trying to work as well.

It would be easy to blame my ADHD for this and, of course, it was a big factor. But I was doing nothing to stop the cycle and manage my symptoms. Now I am much more aware and compassionate with myself, and therefore with others. I do simple things like not scheduling calls when I know the gardener is coming, or taking calls in my car instead. When an unexpected distraction interrupts me, I take three deep breaths and either remove myself from the environment or change the task I am doing, and I break the cycle before I can spiral into panic and anger.

At the time, there weren't a lot of people besides Grant and my assistant (and the gardener, unfortunately) who knew how stressed I was. I spent all my time and energy on work and travel and anything that felt separate from the idea of home. As time went on and Grant continued to decline traveling with me or investing his time and interest in my business, the more I pulled away from him and our life together. The resentment built up slowly, and so did my life away from him. I had groups of friends that Grant had never met, hobbies and routines that he knew nothing about, and countless small moments that he wasn't a part of. I felt safer creating a life without Grant, a life where I felt he could never abandon me.

A few months into this, I got home from yet another trip to New York and went right back to work. I don't think I even looked up from my laptop until hours later, when I went to the bathroom and saw that I was bleeding pretty heavily. I went to the doctor and found out, to my shock, that I was miscarrying. I was only about two months along and had no idea that I was pregnant.

Learning that I was losing a baby I hadn't even known existed was a shock to the system. I had gone to the doctor without telling Grant, so when I got home he still had no idea what was happening. I walked inside and went straight to bed while Grant followed me to our bedroom. He sat on the edge of our bed as I climbed under our crisp white duvet.

"Are you okay?" he asked.

I just shook my head no, feeling my tears well up.

"I was pregnant. I mean, we had a miscarriage," I said as I started to cry, registering the shock on Grant's face. He leaned forward and pulled me into a tight hug.

"Oh, Jace," he said as I cried into his neck.

"I'm sorry," I told him in between sobs. "I'm so sorry."

Grant pulled back to look at me. "What are you sorry for?" he asked.

"I don't know," I said honestly. "I just feel like I let you down."

I didn't get out of bed for a week. I had been going and going and going, and it felt like all of a sudden the merry-go-round just stopped. I was left feeling absolutely nothing. Love, expectation, hope, inspiration, and excitement were no longer flowing through me. I didn't want to feel anything. To feel something meant to hurt, and why would I want to choose to hurt? I didn't want to do anything or leave the house or even work. Grant tried to engage me and get me out of bed, but he couldn't move me.

Looking back, I still can't explain or really even fully understand why I was so bereft after the miscarriage. Having a baby wasn't even on my radar yet. The pregnancy was not intentional. But a loss is a loss, and it still left a void. Losing something that I hadn't even known I'd wanted highlighted how lonely I really felt traveling the world without Grant, how hollow faking it both at work and at home really made me feel.

After I had been in bed for about a week, my brother showed up in my room one day. Justin had moved to LA about a year before Grant and I had gotten married, but we didn't see each other very often, and it definitely wasn't like him to just pop by. Through my fog, I realized that Grant, feeling unable to help me, must have called him.

"Come on, get up," he told me, brusquely pulling my covers aside. "We're going out."

"What? No!" I pulled the covers back onto me like a child fighting with her mom about getting up for school.

"We've got tickets to a movie at three." He stared down

at me with his arms crossed, daring me to say no. "You have twenty minutes to get ready."

I realized that it would be easier to get up and go to the movies than to fight. I wanted to stay in bed, hiding under the covers, where I was safe with my emptiness. I didn't want to move forward because that meant acknowledging that life had to go on. But the look in Justin's eyes meant that he wouldn't take no for an answer. I had no choice but to move forward.

Justin and I saw *About Time*, a beautiful romantic fantasy, and it was somehow just what I needed. The next week, I went out and bought a keyboard and taught myself to play a song from the movie. Sitting in our dark living room next to the fireplace, I pecked away at that keyboard for hours at a time.

Like the stages of grief, the stages of learning a new song are stop-and-go. Many times, I sat in the chair with my fingertips kissing the keys in silence, my eyes tearless. But after a few days, I was able to play the entire song from start to finish. The first time I played the song in its entirety, I smiled, maybe for the first time since the miscarriage. The second time I played it, I had to stop before the end as tears began to flood from my eyes.

I have since played that song hundreds of times. Every time I play it, I secretly dedicate it to our loss. You never fully heal from the loss of a child, but I learned how to carry the grief along with me.

Grant and I finally talked about the miscarriage a few days later, early in the morning as we sat on the couch drinking coffee.

"Should we try for real?" Grant asked me as I stared out the window at an empty hummingbird feeder.

I looked at him, startled. "For a baby?"

"Yeah," he said earnestly. "I know we said we'd wait until later, but after going through this, I wondered if it was something you wanted now."

I hadn't really thought about it. I had simply been grieving. But my answer was clear. "I don't know, Grant," I told him. "Let's maybe hold off a bit."

"Okay, I agree," Grant said, looking down at his coffee. "But someday, though?"

"Yeah, sure," I said, reaching my arm around to the back of his neck. "Just not right now."

We moved on, and I felt that we were truly on the same page about what we both wanted. But somehow, in the mysterious way that losses sometimes do, the whole experience left a space between us. I went on about my business, subconsciously trying to fill that void with more work, more travel, more of everything. I started to branch out from New York and pitch brands on content that I would shoot in other cities around the world. Then I reached out to fashion houses in those cities and set up meetings to start building relationships and fill the time when I was there.

Soon, I was traveling each month to New York, Paris, and London. It was isolating and lonely to be traveling so much alone, but I felt a thrill when I started getting invited to international fashion week shows and events. I filled my cup with these small victories. It was better than being home, sitting on the couch, feeling suffocated, and not knowing why.

But I still wanted more. I dreamed up an idea to go to Sydney for Australian Fashion Week to meet with the Zimmermann team and shoot at Bondi Beach. I was initially drawn to Zimmermann when I discovered them at Barneys New York. It felt like such a small brand in the US at the time, one that only I knew about, and I wanted to be one of the first bloggers to get on their radar.

After the long and exhausting flight, I met with the sisters who had founded Zimmermann, Nicky and Simone. When I arrived at their offices, they couldn't believe that I had flown all the way out there alone. Our meeting turned into lunch and then a tour of their factory and then an afternoon of shopping. I think they were taking pity on me. Over lunch, our waiter overheard me saying that I was in Sydney for the first time. "Oh, look out for the monkeys in the park a few blocks over," he said in his adorable accent. "They live in the trees and they'll jump onto you if you walk underneath."

I was horrified, but Nicky and Simone nodded and laughed along, and I forgot all about it until later that night. I was all dressed up in a floral midi skirt and black bodysuit, walking through the park on the way back to the hotel from an opera I'd gone to by myself. My heart was racing the entire time as I kept my eyes on the trees that hung overhead. There were so many strange animals around. It didn't seem out of the question that a monkey was about to land on my head.

I arrived at the hotel intact. As soon as I was in my room, I took off my heels and sat on a chair, looking out through the floor-to-ceiling window at my view of the harbor, and called Grant.

"It's so strange here," I told him. "The people are great, but it's so different. There are all these animals I've never seen before. Apparently, there are monkeys here that live in trees and will jump out and attack you for no reason."

Grant laughed quietly. "Come on, Jace," he said. "That's just a story they tell tourists to scare them."

"Oh," I said quietly, feeling silly. "You're probably right."

"Listen, I have some bad news," he said calmly. "I finished up our taxes and you owe like sixty grand."

I felt my stomach drop, and I struggled to catch my next breath.

"What?" I asked him. "What do you mean? *Sixty?*"

I didn't know anything about taxes. In the past, my employers had always withheld them, and this was my first year making any sort of significant income through the blog. But I had invested every dollar I made back into the business. I had just gone through an extremely expensive website redesign and had been investing in hiring professional photographers to take pictures for the blog when I traveled. I know this all sounds rather privileged, and it was, but the way I saw it, the more money I threw back into my business, the more money I'd eventually make.

"Come on, Jace, everyone has to pay taxes," Grant said plainly. "If your employer doesn't withhold, then you have to pay at the end of the year. What did you expect?"

"I don't know," I replied honestly. "I had no idea."

I was shaking and thought I might actually throw up, but Grant somehow remained calm. One of the most attractive things about him, and one reason I initially fell in love with Grant, was his ability to stay calm in any situation.

"We'll figure it out," he told me. "You don't have to pay it all at once. We'll come up with a payment plan when you get home." Sure enough, he had heard the anxiety rising in my voice, and he was able to calm me down immediately. It wasn't that Grant didn't feel stressed or let down by my accounting error. He just didn't let the situation derail his emotions or let his emotions control his reaction like I did.

I hung up the phone and looked down at the opera skirt I'd spent three hundred and fifty dollars on so I could feature it on the blog, feeling quite ridiculous. Grant and I still wanted to buy a house and have a family when the time was right. And instead of saving, I'd been running around the world like a fool.

Without wasting another minute, I scooped my hair up into a ponytail, changed into sweats, and pulled out my laptop. Instead of sleeping that night, I stayed up and created an Excel spreadsheet with every detail of each project I had in the pipeline, from timing to deliverables and payment details, to determine how I was going to pay off the tax bill. I started off with the outstanding income owed to me from brands. After I completed a sponsored post, I always sent out an invoice for my fee, which took anywhere from thirty to ninety days to get paid. Since I hadn't been tracking anything, I had no idea how much income I could expect over the next few months. Every month was a little bit different, depending on how many projects I booked, but laying it all out gave me a good idea of my average income month to month.

Next, I looked at my expected commission rate for the next year. When I first started the blog, my commissions from rewardStyle were a couple thousand dollars each month, which was great. Now they would have been enough to live off of full-time if I didn't spend them on trips and outfits. I ran the numbers of various scenarios to see how much I needed to save to pay the taxes I owed and to plan ahead for the next year's taxes. I came up with an aggressive plan to put aside half of my overall income for taxes. This meant I would need to cut back significantly on eating out, shopping, and paying out of pocket for travel.

I started by changing my flight to head back to LA a few days early and cut down the cost of my trip to Australia. For the next year, I focused on doing partnerships for trade. I asked brands to let me borrow clothes and hotels to put me up in exchange for posts. When I needed wine, I reached out to wine companies asking if they wanted to send me a few cases in exchange for a post. When I wanted to furnish my bedroom, I reached out to Crate and Barrel to see if we could do a trade. I bartered everything I possibly could. It helped me pay off my debt and forge relationships with different categories of brands.

Taking control of our finances also allowed us to finally buy a house the next year by finding one that basically no one else wanted. It was small and old and needed a ton of work. I wish I could say that I fell in love with that house right away. When Grant first brought me there, I walked in and saw the lime-green floors and lime-green walls and wanted to walk right back out. But Grant had a vision for how to transform the house, and he won me over with images of what it would ultimately look like. Once we drew up the plans with Grant's brother, an architect, I got excited, especially when I saw how big my closet was going to be!

While Grant spent the next eight months gutting the house down to studs, we moved into a loft that he had renovated through his company. Seeing an opportunity to cover the project on my blog, I decided to film a series called Home Sweet Damsel about the house renovation. I saw it as the perfect marriage of Grant's passion for real-estate development and my world of fashion and design, but Grant hated being on camera, and I worried that the whole thing felt stilted.

I was traveling so much that Grant and I spent very little time together off camera, and I constantly worried that people watching would pick up on the underlying tension between us. I tried to draw from that tension to create little on-screen moments between us that felt cheeky and comical. But we were faking it in those cute little videos. It's so clear to me when I look back at them now. I knew it at the time and was obsessed with the idea that people might see through us and intuit that something was wrong. But instead of addressing what was missing, I put my energy into creating even more of a facade.

I hadn't heard from Robin at Banana Republic in a while when she reached out from a new email address, asking if I could meet and hear about the new company she was working at. Over lunch at Cookshop, she told me that she was at an agency that represented Cotton Inc.

"I really want to talk them into doing something with you," she told me. "The whole cotton-farmer's-daughter angle could be so cool. But they've never done anything with an influencer before. We'll have to get creative."

At first, I wasn't sure how it would work. Cotton Inc. was a nonprofit organization that supported the cotton industry, not a brand or a fashion label. But as I thought about it on the flight back to LA, I realized that it was the perfect opportunity to teach people how the clothes they wore were made. It was the first time I really contemplated the intimate connection between my dad's career and my own. The clothes I posted about were made of the very stuff he grew with his own hands. It would be so special to share with the world the process of how cotton went from my dad's farm to the store to my blog.

I went home and put together the most grown-up pitch of my career, with multiple verticals and posting strategies and a video component that I would fly back home to Texas to shoot. When Cotton Inc. said yes, it felt very much like the moment I'd gotten the job at Oprah. It was a big deal—my biggest payday yet—and, just as important, I knew that my family would be proud of me.

Flying home to shoot this video felt completely different from the Levi's shoot I'd done just four years earlier. I felt so much more confident about what I was doing, but I was also that much more obsessive and controlling about every little detail. I spent three hours in the blazing Texas sun making sure the dirt smudge on my white cotton off-the-shoulder top was absolutely perfect. As I changed outfits three different times in the 110-degree heat index with dust from harvest season flying violently in the air, we hopped from farm to farm across San Patricio County to the Midway Gin and Grain Co-op for a full tour on how cotton is harvested.

In between shots, I snapped at Grant and rolled my eyes when the videographer asked for another take of a shot I assumed we had already gotten. I got annoyed by my mom as she questioned my outfit choices, and I barked at my assistant to hold the mic boom higher and higher. But I wasn't as short-tempered with my dad. He was a big part of the shoot, taking me around the cotton fields just as he had done the first time he'd taught me all about the family business when I was a child. It felt like we were making up for all the lost time in between.

I knew that my own unhealthy behaviors were starting to creep up and that this wasn't who I was at my core. At the same time, obsessing over tiny details and working hard was paying off. As I was controlling more of my outfits, more of the camera angles, and more of the shoots I was doing, I was getting more likes, more clicks, and more deals than ever. I told myself that while my work may have been an addiction, it wasn't a *bad* addiction like one to drugs or alcohol. I was nothing like my dad, clutching his bottle of vodka on his way to rehab. But the more I expected perfection from myself, the more I required it from everyone around me.

In New York that year for fashion week, I was doing an Instagram takeover for Tory Burch on the morning of her show. I loved getting this type of work, but then having to get my hair and makeup done and go on Instagram Live in front of millions of people always felt fake and over-the-top. That morning, I was waiting in my hotel room for my hair and makeup team, wearing a white fluffy robe and clutching a mug of room service coffee.

"Where are they?" I asked my assistant, checking the time on my phone. "I have to go live in fifteen minutes!"

"Let me check what time we said they'd arrive," Haleigh said, scrolling through her phone.

When I saw the look on her face moments later, I knew exactly what had happened.

"You didn't book them," I said.

She looked up at me as if she'd seen a ghost. "I'm so sorry," she whispered. "I don't know how this happened."

Haleigh was sick over her mistake, and kept begging me not to fire her. The ironic thing is I wasn't even that mad. I quickly did my own makeup and got dressed in a matching plaid-on-plaid Tory Burch suit and moved on with my jam-packed day. But I silently registered the fact that there was a reason Haleigh was so scared.

Months prior, I had received an email from the Louis Vuitton team saying they never received a bag that I had borrowed on my trip to New York. I'd phoned the EDITION Hotel, where I'd stayed, and spoke to not one, not two, but three managers in a sarcastic tone, trying to track down the missing bag. I had left it with the concierge for pickup, but somehow it had gone missing.

"Well, if it's your job to fix it, then maybe you should do *your* job," I snarked over the phone. Unfortunately, Haleigh was no stranger to my nasty and controlling hold on things.

Let me be clear: Looking back on my behavior, I know that I was acting like an asshole, and I feel terrible. I was driven by the need to be perfect and to succeed at all costs, and I didn't realize how much it was affecting the people around me. We were all becoming more successful the more I tightened the reins, and I was so afraid of losing control if I loosened that grip. I wish I could go back and tell that Jacey to take a deep breath and chill out, that she'd be more successful and far happier if she could find a way to act like her kind and loving self.

Going through this, however, has given me insight into why some people can act so cruelly to others, particularly on social media. Behind every nasty comment on Instagram, every hurtful word someone uses to describe another person, and every mean look a person gives to another, there lies a world of pain and fear. My eye rolls and snide comments pointing out that someone else wasn't doing their job correctly were reflections of my own inner child telling herself that she wasn't good enough.

To that inner child, losing control meant losing my facade. It meant that my dad would go pick up the bottle and keep drinking. It meant that everyone could see through the filters and walls that I had put up around me to hide the fact that I actually felt quite lost and like I had no idea what I was really doing. I was so determined not to let that cover-up slip that I unfortunately locked myself into these bad behaviors for quite some time.

That fashion week was extra stressful because for the first time I was doing the "full circuit," which meant I was attending fashion week back-to-back in New York,

London, Paris, and Milan. I was gone for a total of five weeks, and during that time Grant was moving us into the new house, which was finally ready.

Those five weeks included some moments of extreme highs. I was invited backstage at Dior for the first time to cover the hair and makeup part of the show. To get in, I had to walk through the herds of street-style photographers toward the entrance before being greeted by five men with clipboards who double-checked to see if I was on the backstage list. When I was finally granted access, it felt like I had won the lottery.

I felt giddy when I returned to the hotel that night. I had a gorgeous rooftop penthouse at The Peninsula Hotel in Paris that was truly fit for a queen. But five weeks is a long time to be away from home.

Grant met me in London halfway through the trip, but instead of a happy reunion, it felt as forced as the Home Sweet Damsel videos. I had been experiencing so much of my life without him, and it felt like the one we shared together had grown very small. I sat across from him at the Four Seasons Hotel Hampshire underneath layers and layers of items from high-end fall collections, along with layers and layers of unspoken truths. We simply had nothing to say.

After five long weeks away, I wasn't returning home. I was going to a new house. Walking in with my luggage, I took in the unbelievable transformation Grant had accomplished. What had once been a lime-green laminate-floored starter home was now an inspired renovation that looked like it belonged in a West Elm ad or an HGTV episode. It was beautiful. Grant had nailed it, and I was impressed. But it wasn't lost on me that I was touring our new house alone. We had our rule, and I hadn't expected Grant to pick me up at the airport, but I had hoped he'd be waiting to meet me at the door with a kiss. He was in the shower, and I greeted William and Polly with kisses and dog treats instead.

Once I settled in, I curled up on the couch with the dogs and my phone, but I didn't check Instagram. I just sat there. A wave of gratitude came over me for all the incredible experiences I had just had: amazing travels, high-end clothing, and now I found myself sitting in a beautiful house that was my home. I took a very deep breath in appreciation of these accomplishments and the goodness in my life. But it also felt muted by the absence in my heart.

During that time, I was focused on what everyone around me was doing. But the person that I was the least connected with was myself. I wanted to be happy in my marriage, but I didn't have the tools. I wanted to laugh and live a light-hearted life, but all I could feel was sadness.

Many years later, I learned the difficult lesson that I could choose to be miserable, or I could choose to be strong. The amount of effort that goes into being either happy or sad is the same. I felt like I was unfixable, so I looked for evidence that other people or situations were unfixable, too. I was focusing on things that I disliked in others because, at the time, these were the things that I hated about myself. I could have saved a lot of time and heartache if I had just been brave enough to work on fixing me.

7

Rock Bottom

BY 2015, I WAS IN NEW YORK EVERY OTHER WEEK.
When I was there for meetings, I stayed at the Four Seasons, where I found peonies on my nightstand, but during
fashion week everyone stayed at the Empire.

The Empire Hotel was located right across the street
from Lincoln Center, where fashion week was held. I don't
know what the hotel was like during a typical week, but
during fashion week it was a scene. Every blogger and his
or her entire team turned their hotel rooms into dressing
rooms, hair and makeup suites, and even production cen-
ters. *E! News* taped their coverage of fashion week from the
Empire's roof. It was the fashion week hub. And the crosswalk outside that led to Lincoln Center was the location

of "the walk"—how and when and with whom attendees arrived at shows during fashion week and later made their way back out onto the street.

No one really talks about it or admits it, but there was nothing accidental or spontaneous about the walk, and this was true long before bloggers even existed. For years, editors and other fashion industry titans planned out their outfits, the timing of their arrivals, and even whom they walked into the show with weeks in advance, all so it could be caught on camera by the street-style photographers waiting outside the shows.

Before blogging, these photos would show up in the *Sunday Times*, future issues of *Vogue*, *Vanity Fair*, and other fashion magazines, setting the trends for the coming season just as much as the items appearing on the runway themselves. By 2015, bloggers were a huge part of the equation. Fashion photographers capturing the show were shooting us as we arrived, too. Plus, we often hired our own photographers, and we posted these images on our social media and blogs, making an even greater and more immediate impact than much of the official fashion reporting in newspapers and magazines. Some bloggers even hired their photographers to act as street-style photographers outside of shows, just to cause a stir. The flood of photographers would inevitably follow the lead of these hired guns, resulting in even more photos being snapped of the bloggers who hired them.

When it was up to fashion magazines alone to present these images, it was at the discretion of an editor. We've all seen *The Devil Wears Prada*, right? That person selected which photos of which outfits by which labels to present to the public. When readers purchased the items they saw in magazines, it led stores to buy more of these items and brands to create more of them. Often, more affordable brands followed, making similar but lower-cost versions of those items for the general populace. This caused a huge downstream effect on the entire industry and is how trends typically began. Those editors therefore had a disproportionate amount of power over the entire industry.

Blogging changed all that. No one told us what to post. There were no gatekeepers standing in between us and our readers. The images we chose to share went straight to our readers' eyeballs. Either consciously or subconsciously, they made purchasing decisions based on what we posted, meaning we had a direct influence over the industry in the same way that magazines once did.

Editors, of course, hated this. There were so many articles written at around this time slamming bloggers and saying that we didn't belong at fashion shows. I have to admit, there were times when I questioned our worthiness myself. But over time and through selling the crap out of the clothes that designers had us wearing to their shows, we finally proved ourselves. Editors still hated us, though.

Our influence compounded when bloggers decided to work together. Think about it. If one blogger shared an image of herself walking into a fashion week show wearing a particular outfit, only her followers would see it. But if two popular bloggers were photographed together in seemingly fortuitous but highly coordinated outfits and both of them shared those images, they were seen by twice as many eyeballs. Potentially twice as many people would choose what to buy and wear accordingly, but only if we were working with another blogger who had roughly the same number of followers as we did. So, it often seemed like who we were seen walking in and out of shows with was just as important as what we were wearing and what shows we were attending to begin with.

With all of us staying at the Empire, it was easy to text a friend and say, I'm walking down in five; meet me in the lobby, or to pop into someone's room to see what they were wearing and throw on an item in the same color. That way, you became a whole trend walking into the show together.

One small example of this is a simple basket-weave wooden tote bag from Cult Gaia. When the bag first hit the market, it didn't make much of an impact. But when several bloggers (including yours truly) discovered the bag and were photographed together carrying it, it became the "it" bag that girls everywhere suddenly wanted. The industry followed, and now there are similar wooden totes available at every price point, starting at twenty dollars.

I'm not trying to overinflate my importance or the importance of blogging in general. After all, we're just a bunch of girls bouncing around the world taking frivolous selfies. But fashion week has always been about forecasting and reporting on trends. What bloggers like me were doing at this time was throwing into question who exactly was setting those trends. Was it the fashion houses, the magazine editors, or the bloggers? If women were changing their shopping habits based on what they saw bloggers wearing into the shows just as much as (or more than) what was actually presented on the runway, that meant we were real players in the industry with real power.

Even major fashion photographers were taking note and snapping pictures of fashion bloggers walking in and out of shows. I will never forget the day the infamous *New York Times* street-style photographer Bill Cunningham first snapped an image of me. I called Grant and said, "Guess who just took my photo?"

He immediately replied, "Bill." Even Grant knew Bill's name; that's how big of a deal he was.

Of course, this influence came with a dark side. When it seems like what you look like, what you're wearing, and who you're walking next to really matters, the situation is ripe for pettiness and competition to flourish. I found myself on the receiving end of this for years.

For a long time, I had fewer followers than other bloggers who were considered at my level. My readers were loyal and my conversion rate was high (meaning my followers frequently bought the items I posted about), but all anybody saw when they clicked on my Instagram was my number of followers. So, it took a long time for me to find myself among the chosen few bloggers who planned to walk in and out of events together. Trivial as it seems, who you walked into a fashion show with really did impact the trajectory of your career.

When I was starting out, I told brands that I was happy to stand in the back, and I meant it. As my career progressed, I was terribly grateful to find myself working my way row by row up to the front at shows. I bit my tongue when a popular blogger walked in with her assistant, a publicist, and a whole team, stood with her back to me, and then asked me to scooch back to the second row so she could take my hard-earned spot when the show started. I bit it again when I was at the front of a long line for a tiny elevator after the show and that same blogger came up to me from the back of the line and acted like my best friend. She chatted with me until the very moment the elevator doors opened and then she and her entire team rushed in, leaving no room for me inside. I understood that this was part of the song and dance of the industry. If I wanted to be a part of it, I had to play along. But some of these slights hurt more than others.

The first Christmas in our new house, Grant and I threw a holiday party. We invited forty of our closest friends to an indoor/outdoor quintessential LA house party, complete with spiked punch, hipster holiday tunes on vinyl, and a blow-up Santa in the front yard. We even put Santa hats on Polly and William for the occasion.

A month or so before the party, I'd gone out to lunch with a fellow blogger whom I'll call Taylor. We'd known each other for a while and had bonded over the fact that we were both from Texas. Over lunch at Toast, wearing a matching gingham top and skirt, Taylor was visibly upset.

"What's wrong?" I asked her. "Are you okay?"

She shook her head and looked like she was fighting back tears. "Oh, I was just reading *The Forum*," she told me. I stared at her blankly, with no idea what she was talking about. "It's a website that started by attacking mommy bloggers," she explained, "but I guess they've branched

out. All of these haters are on there just ripping me apart."
She paused to take a breath. "I bet you have a page on
there, too." She pulled out her phone as if she was going
to show me.

"No, no, no," I said, waving her phone away with my
hand. "I don't want to see all that!" I still had a thin skin
and took negative comments on my blog very personally. I
knew how awful it would feel to know about a hate forum
with a page dedicated to me.

But Taylor wouldn't hear me. "Let me just look," she
said, pulling *The Forum* up on her phone. I speared some
lettuce onto my fork and tried my best to ignore what was
happening across the table from me. "Hmm," Taylor said
as she continued scrolling. "You're not on there." I ex-
haled deeply. "I can't believe it," she said, scrunching her
eyebrows together before looking up at me. "Well, maybe
one day when you have as many followers as me."

I let the comment slide, and we moved on to other top-
ics, but this conversation was on my mind a few weeks
later at our Christmas party. It was a fun and slightly rau-
cous time. I got a little bit tipsy and smoked a couple of
cigarettes outside with my best friends from E!, Catt and
Ashley. (Don't @ me. I don't smoke anymore.) There were
about ten other bloggers at the party, including Taylor.
Everyone seemed to get along and have fun. Grant's best
friends from high school all stayed long after most of my
industry friends left. We ended up cranking the heat on
the pool for a late-night dip and ordering pizza at 2:00 a.m.

Shortly after the New Year, I was at my desk in full-
on hustle mode. My office was in the old garage to our

house that the owners had converted into a soundproof studio, complete with a light tan carpet and two white French doors leading out to the back pool. At the time, it was trendy to mismatch various sizes and types of art into a gallery wall, which was exactly what I had done in my office. The frames were all white, but inside the art pieces varied from magazine printouts of Chanel ads, photography by my friend Gray Malin, and a few illustrations of bulldogs, lipsticks, and handbags.

I had an oversized desk from CB2, with an oatmeal-colored sofa from World Market directly in front of it. Many evenings, you would find me sitting on the sofa playing *Halo* on my Xbox 360. What can I say? I'm a computer nerd through and through.

Before I fired up a round of *Halo*, I had just made my new list of goals for the year and was checking on my latest stats when I noticed a sudden influx of traffic on the blog from a new source: *The Forum*. My stomach dropped to the floor as I realized this likely meant there was now a page dedicated to me. Otherwise, why would people be funneling into the blog from there?

Don't click on it, Jacey, I said to myself. *There is no good that can come from this.* But I just couldn't stop my fingers from clicking on that link.

The first few comments I saw were hurtful, but they were the same types of things I'd already been hearing for years:

She has one hell of a jaw on her. *Yes, true. I can't deny that.*

Her angled jaw really bothers me. *So sorry to offend you. This is just my face.*

Look into retinol, hyaluronic acid, and nicotine gum, tootsie, it will do your collagen a world of good. *Sigh, yes, I am starting to see wrinkles in the mirror. Thanks for noticing.*

Her personality puts her bad taste to shame. *Ouch.*

These comments definitely stung, but I tried to push down those emotions. I worked my way back to the very first comment that launched the thread (yes, I totally did this), and the tone shifted. These comments were from someone who claimed that she knew me personally, had been at parties with me, and had insights into my personal relationships. This person claimed to have seen me chain-smoking (not true), that I grew up with a silver spoon in my mouth (ha, not true), and most offensive, that I had married Grant for money. (Please. If I were marrying for money, I would have gone for *money*.) Other commenters jumped all over this thread, but the initial post hurt the most:

Most relationships she has with other bloggers are fake. She makes fun of everyone behind their backs but maintains a relationship to get more followers. I just think she needs to be outed for who she really is—a chain-smoking, mean, entitled little rich girl. Jacey, you're just a gold-digging spoiled bitch.

I took a deep breath and told myself not to let this affect me. But the room started to spin around me as I kept reading until I had seen every single comment, like I was picking at a scab that I knew would only leave a scar. It was obvious to me that Taylor had started the thread, after I'd befriended and opened my home to her, and I felt deeply violated. These people were attacking not just me, but also Grant and even my parents, who hadn't asked for this. I was the one who had chosen to put my entire life up for display: the good, the bad, and the apparently ugly jaw. And now every negative thought I had ever had about myself and my family was staring me right in the face, like a mirror that revealed only flaws.

Over the next few weeks, I became obsessed with *The Forum*. I checked it constantly. I took each of the bloggers I had invited to the holiday party out to lunch and then asked pointed questions and tried to use my intuition to sense if they were the one who'd started the thread. Taylor was the only one who declined my invitation, which told me everything I needed to know.

Grant saw me spiraling and tried to get me to stop reading the hateful comments, but I ignored him. I spent a lot of time ignoring him in general. It was so much easier to do this than it was to try to understand why we weren't connecting like we used to.

I felt like I was back in high school, being attacked by the mean girls while the foundation of my life at home was crumbling beneath my feet. And just like I did back then, I responded by running away from the problems while at the same time leaning into the pain. It felt like I was losing control, so I gripped even tighter to the reins of control and perfectionism. Those comments made me question my self-worth, my choices, my work, and my life's meaning, so I put up even more boundaries and filters so that no one could see what was really happening behind closed doors. It was too hard to face the reality, so I ran.

Running away from my problems was nothing new for me. In high school, I ran for the track team. I was already on the swim team doing laps at the pool four times a day, and running became another escape and excuse to just keep moving. I stayed out of the house as much as possible, while my dad's drinking and my parents' fighting were both at all-time highs.

When I was at home, I was completely tied up in the drama. As soon as I heard voices being raised, I'd race to defend my mom. As soon as I heard the clink of ice hitting the bottom of a glass, I raced into the kitchen to beg my dad to stop.

The mornings around our house, however, were relatively quiet. As soon as I got up, I headed off to the pool for my first swim of the day. Later in life, when I started practicing yoga, I learned how important it was to me to take care of my greater "yin" energy (aka my feminine energy) versus my "yang" (masculine) energy. Our yin energy is intuitive, creative, sensitive, and receiving, and our yang energy is confident, protective, assertive, and giving.

I dived into the swimming pool four times a day during high school not just because I had the goal of being an All-State Swimmer. It was my body's instinctive need to cool off all the heated "yang" energy I had pulsing through me during that time. It gave my mind space to finally be free from distractions so I could tune in to being present in a moment when nothing mattered except my freestyle stroke.

Now my frequent flights and trips to New York were my escape, and I upped the pace of my international travel even more. Rather than dive into healing my wounds, I foolishly thought I could solve my problems through all these lavish trips. I wasn't worried about Grant. I figured he would always be there when I returned. So, I ran, just like I had in high school, and the more I ran, the more Grant stayed still. His coping mechanism was to bury his head in the sand instead of facing the music, and my coping mechanism was to keep moving and live with no regrets, even if that meant hurting the ones I loved most.

Luckily (or not), evolving trends in the industry aided my escape. REVOLVE, a trendy retailer, started sending groups of influencers on trips together with tons of picturesque events and meals so they would post pictures of themselves wearing their clothes and tagging the brand with the hashtag #RevolveAroundTheWorld. I participated in one of their first events in The Hamptons as one of eight bloggers who shared a house for the weekend. We took photos of ourselves poolside, on giant flamingo-shaped rafts, eating lavish meals, and at the weekend's multiple parties.

I shared a room with a male blogger named Isaac and my friend Courtney, who worked at *Who What Wear*, and we had a blast. Grant didn't flinch at the fact that I was sharing a hotel room and constantly posting photos of myself with Isaac. And there was a small part of me that wondered what it would really take to wake him up.

This was the first of many #RevolveAroundTheWorld trips, and it was fun, but the whole experience left me feeling icky. It felt fake to present pictures of us hanging out together like the "cool kids" in school, especially when the

Top Left:
Easter Sunday with
my parents and Justin

Top Right:
My younger years with
the greatest style icon
I know: my mom

Left:
At my first stock show
holding a second-place
ribbon for my pigs

Me and Justin
with our dogs,
Sam and Libby,
on Duprie Farms

Right: Shannon and
I before Champagne
Thursday night,
and I'm carrying
my pink Chanel

Far Right: Me, Gia
and Shannon at a
sorority fundraiser

Heading to our
sorority formal event
senior year of college

Left: My family visit to *The Oprah Winfrey Show*

Bottom: At my twenty-fifth birthday party—our first photo together

Right: Glam squad for Catt on the roof of Empire Hotel at New York Fashion Week

Far Right: In Bali on our honeymoon where we came up with the idea for my blog (2011)

With my family the night before Grant and I got married

Right: In our condo shooting with Levi's for my first ever campaign

Far Right: Shoot against the famous pink blogger wall in Los Angeles, and my first time shooting with a professional photographer

Photo Credit: Lauren Ross

Left: First ever New York Fashion Week, walking to BCBG show

Photo Credit: Michael Dumler

Far Left: Ashley and I on step and repeat for Bvlgari event

Left: At my first home office shooting for a magazine at my desk

Left: Snuggling up with William and Polly the week after my miscarriage

Right: Wearing Valentino for the Luisa Via Roma editorial shoot

Photo Credit: Hana Lê Van

Far Right: Zimmermann show with Ashley and Courtney

Shooting a Tiffany & Co. campaign in April 2017 with my team: Haleigh, Felicia and Maria

Photo Credit: Felicia Lasala

On my way to Paris Fashion Week

Me working in my office the day we got the Amazon deal

Far Left: At my first Dior show in Paris

Left: Me and Haleigh on the Tom Ford trip in Positano

Far Left: Grant's first Instagram post on his way to New York with our dog, Polly

Left: Grant at his first fashion show, sitting right behind me in second row

Before the ICONS party when Grant made me laugh in a quick moment caught by our photographer

Photo Credit: Frankie Marin

Right: The Chanel ring Grant gave me at The Polo Bar

Far Right: With Catt at The Polo Bar after a fashion week party

Right: During the busiest New York Fashion Week season of my career, shooting a campaign for Carolina Herrera

Left: With Tory Burch before her show in New York

Left: Front row at Zimmermann with fellow influencers and bloggers

Bottom: Walking to my first Chanel show in Paris

Right: With my
two fashion friends
Courtney Trop and
Charlotte Groeneveld
at the Chanel
couture show

Far Right: Outside
the backstage area
at Dior

Right: With Dad,
shooting in the fields
for the Cotton Inc.
project

On our way to the
black-tie gala with
Dior, dressed in Dior

Far Left: After several shoots, we finally decided on a mirror selfie for the Instagram pregnancy announcement

Left: Bump shot in my final trimester

My girls coming over to cheer me up during my pregnancy

Far Left: Front row at Tom Ford, feeling very pregnant, with Arielle Charnas and Charlotte Groeneveld

Left: At the Chanel show, feeling very pregnant and unstylish

The first photo of
me with June

Right: The morning
after June was born

Far Right: Summer
in Italy, posing by the
pool in Summersalt

Me, Catt and Lina
taking in the
Florence sunset
(2019)

Sitting in
the By Damsel
pop-up store for
the *Vogue* feature

**Photo Credit:
Eric Doolin**

One of the only family photos we took during quarantine

**Photo Credit:
Morgan Pansing**

Our Christmas card in 2020

**Photo Credit:
Monica Wang**

In Concan, Texas, celebrating Dad's fifteen-year sobriety

Far Left: Blue beaded necklace Dad gave me at rehab

Left: My parents with June and Finn, Fourth of July, 2021

June and me in Concan, Texas, with my family for Fourth of July

xoxo jacey

whole trip was really about sales. It did succeed in generating sales, though.

On my next trip to New York, I was brainstorming at lunch with the marketing director at UGG. I suggested they send a group of bloggers to Aspen and shoot us wearing the next season's collection. UGG loved the idea and gave me the entire budget. I coordinated the whole project—hiring a photographer, inviting and paying the other girls, scouting locations, and so on. It was like shooting a movie, and I loved obsessing over every detail.

The fellow bloggers on this trip seemed more in tune with their personal style than I was, and I saw how carefully they calculated the photos they posted. I learned so much from them about how to layer, pose for photos, and look effortless while doing so. I loved learning new ways to do old tricks. If the people on the REVOLVE trip were at the "cool kids" table in high school, these were the girls who were at the even cooler table in the corner.

Next up was a trip to Positano, Italy, with Tom Ford to promote their newest line of fragrances. They invited two bloggers from each of several countries on this trip, and I was one of the lucky two who were chosen from the US. It was an honor. Always looking for an excuse to travel, I added a three-day layover beforehand in Paris, where I met with the teams at Louis Vuitton, Dior, and a few other brands.

For the Paris leg of the trip, The Peninsula put us up in an incredible rooftop suite. We had a large terrace with a picture-perfect view of the Eiffel Tower, a courtyard, and every luxurious amenity you could possibly imagine.

When I say *we*, no, I am not referring to Grant. I didn't even ask him to come with me on that trip. I felt so resentful toward him during this time that I figured I was better off being without him.

Grant was steady. Yes, he was always there at home, waiting for me to return from my travels. But it didn't feel like he was willing to fight for me. I asked myself why he wasn't more passionate about our relationship, why he didn't mind me flying off every two seconds, and why he wasn't more curious about who I was spending time with when I was gone. The only answer I could come up with was that he just didn't care. So, I told myself not to care in return.

My assistant, Haleigh, came with me to Paris instead, and we leaned heavily into work, hopping around the city, taking as many meetings as I could cram into our schedule, getting good photos, and eating every delicious thing we could find. Inside, I felt incredibly lonely and abandoned, even though I was the one who was running away from Grant instead of the other way around. As usual, I pushed those feelings down and worried more about how it would look to my readers and the haters on *The Forum* that I had taken my assistant with me on this romantic trip instead of my husband.

In Positano, I found myself at yet another luxurious hotel, Il San Pietro. My room had a full wraparound balcony that overlooked the beautiful ocean, which was surrounded by steep cliffs dotted with ancient European homes. It was an unbelievable setting. On our first night, the entire group of bloggers and editors were treated to a multicourse dinner, during which each course was paired with one of five fragrances, creating a unique full sensory experience. The following morning, we took part in a cooking class with the head chef at the hotel, followed by an afternoon at sea.

Dressed for the occasion in a silk burnt-orange Heidi Merrick pajama top, wide vertical-striped pants, and a straw hat, I joined the group for a boat tour around Positano. After lunch, I stripped down to a black one-piece by Solid & Striped and plunged into the water for a grand total of five seconds just to get a good photo to post. It was shockingly cold!

Everything about that trip was beautiful down to the smallest detail. And I was so grateful to be there, to have been chosen, and to get to experience such luxury. This was the kind of trip I never would have been able to imagine growing up in Texas. I had no clue that such luxury even existed! But inside, I was so unhappy.

I know, I know. Poor me. But while I posted pictures of myself having the time of my life in Italy, I felt so incredibly alone. To make things even worse, I heard from a fellow blogger that one of the girls I'd brought to Aspen for the UGG shoot was saying behind my back that I only put that trip together because I had no real friends to travel with. This rumor made no sense. It was a work trip. I knew that in my heart, but all the negative comments coming at me from different directions were breaking me down.

I had no boundaries between my life and my work or any emotional boundaries between myself and my readers, other bloggers, or friends in the industry. And my readers had no boundaries from me, either. One woman I corresponded with daily reached out and told me that she was quitting social media because she realized that she was growing too reliant on our relationship. If I didn't respond to her messages within the same day, she was crushed, and she knew this wasn't healthy.

When I posted about a trip to Florida, one reader showed up at my hotel. Another reader arrived one day at my front door, even though my address wasn't listed anywhere and we'd bought the house anonymously. At one point, even my own ob-gyn asked for a shout-out on Instagram during a routine annual visit.

It saddened me to realize that I had to slowly stop messaging directly with all my readers because these relationships were at the heart of my brand. My favorite part of the job for so long had been connecting with readers. But it was taking up way too much of my time and mental energy. I often spent all day trying to answer questions from my readers, but I never got to them all and then felt terrible about it. Other times, answering one question led to five more.

When readers messaged me about their own heartaches and tragedies, I was honored, but it affected me deeply, and I couldn't turn it off and unplug at the end of the day. My life was my work. The call was coming from inside the house!

And I made it worse for myself. In between all those trips and meetings, I was checking *The Forum*, reading every one of the horrible things that people had to say about me. But I couldn't stop looking. I became addicted to seeing what horrible things people on *The Forum* were saying. They were picking apart the aspects of my life that I was already the most insecure about: my marriage, my looks, and whether or not I even deserved to be a part of this industry. Reading these things left me gutted and doubting my own life and decisions. I tried to go a week or two without checking, but, like any addict, I found myself back on *The Forum* without really knowing how I had gotten there.

I was familiar with this addiction to pain. It was as if feeling something, anything, was better than the loneliness that surrounded me the rest of the time. At least I could direct my feelings toward an awful sentence that someone had written about my frizzy hair and not have to focus on the fact that I hadn't been romantic with my husband for months.

Back in high school, some mornings weren't so quiet. One day, I woke up at 8:00 a.m. to the sounds of my mom screaming at my dad in the driveway, "What the hell is going on here so goddamn early on a Saturday!"

The autopilot inside of me took over, and before I could even think about what I was doing, I found myself outside, violently screaming, too. My hair was a disheveled mess, and I had sleep still stuck in my eyes. My bare feet sank into the rough gravel from the driveway. I sniffed and caught my breath, shifting my long gray nightgown, relishing the pain in my feet.

"I'm so fucking sick of this shit," I cried out as I stormed toward my dad's dark gray Ford pickup truck. Knowing exactly where to find them, I dug out four large handles of vodka, two empty and two nearly empty. I had reached my rock bottom, but my dad was still searching for his. All I wanted was for him to stop drinking. All I begged for was to wake up before school and sit at the kitchen table with my dad and have a sober conversation about school, life, college, and the other worries that weighed down my seventeen-year-old mind.

My request felt simple. I took my anger and disappointment out on the bottles by aggressively slamming them into the ground. As tiny pieces of glass shattered around my bare feet, my dad took a step toward me, as if he wanted to protect me. But the rage that I was unveiling scared him. It scared me, too.

"Why is this so hard?" I yelled as the last bottle crashed to the ground. My aching feet carried me back into the house, walking on the glass and secretly hoping it would cut my feet for dramatic effect. I wanted my dad to feel bad, for him to see firsthand the pain he was putting me through.

Slamming my bedroom door, I locked the handle and passed by the blue ribbons, first-place trophies, megaphones, pageant crowns, and photographs of myself among a group of smiling cheerleaders that were plastered across my bulletin boards. I went into my closet and locked that door behind me, too. And I just sat there, catching my breath and staring up blankly at those wallpapered clouds. An hour could have passed, but I did not move.

Finally, I stood up and made my way into the bathroom. Without hesitation, I searched my drawers to find something sharp. All I came across was a very rough callus remover for at-home pedicures. I sat down on a chair in the bathroom, staring at myself in the mirror with the callus remover in my left hand. I slowly raised the jagged blade to my left cheek, pressing until I began to bleed.

Looking back, if any moment could have given me empathy for my dad, this was it. Many addicts use substances to numb themselves from emotional pain or simply to feel something else. In that moment, I, too, was desperate to feel anything but the anger, hurt, and abandonment that came with my dad choosing those bottles of vodka over me.

The remainder of the day passed just as any other Saturday, with a trip to town to pick up fast food for lunch and intermittent fights between my parents, all of which I mediated. In between, I just waited for the day to end. As the sun set, I made my way across the field in the back of our house to another house about two miles away. One of the other cheerleaders' parents were out of town for the weekend, and she was having a small house party with the popular crowd from high school. Football players, cheerleaders, and other friends from the upper class were all in attendance.

I liked drinking, but I never really got hammered at parties. I was standing off in a corner by the hot tub, sipping a Zima with Jolly Ranchers in it, when a football player I'd had a crush on for months asked me what had happened to my cheek. He was the first person to notice all day, and his attention made me feel a pinch of excitement. He asked if I wanted to go get a late-night burger, and I eagerly hopped into his SUV. Just as we reached the end of the driveway, the car stopped and another football player got in the back seat.

Thinking nothing of it, I leaned back in my seat, and we took off for town. The fastest route included a two-mile cruise down a very dark country road that went near my house. Surrounded by cotton fields, the lights of our small town were faint in the distance. The only signs of life came from the occasional car driving down an adjacent road.

Suddenly, the SUV pulled over into the dirt just off the road. The driver took off his seat belt, leaned over the middle console, and started kissing me. A rush of butterflies swam in my stomach, as I wondered for how long this football player had wanted to kiss me. After a minute, I realized that I had completely forgotten about our additional passenger in the back seat. Just as I started to pull away from the first football player, it hit me that the two upperclassmen might have an agenda.

All of a sudden, football player number two grabbed my head, pulled me into the back seat, and held me there with all his strength. The other one was undoing my pants as my body fought against both of them and my mind raced with possible scenarios. Not knowing how to get out of the situation, I wondered if I should just go along with it, if fighting them off would only make things worse. Sure enough, every time I tried to pull away ever so slightly, they forcefully held me in place. I didn't know what a bad situation I was in until I was in it.

The more seconds that ticked by, the more a boiling fear started to cook me from inside out. The strength to pull away was just as hard emotionally as it was physically. Part of me felt that I deserved to be violated in this way and worried that if I ran away the football players would tell everyone what had happened or make up a story that was even worse. But my fear won out above all else. Shaking and desperately looking for a way out, in one swift move I blocked off the grip on my head and escaped out the passenger door.

I ran as far as I could into the cotton fields until my legs couldn't carry me any longer. The Lang farm connected the land where the party was held to our family farm. I collapsed into the dirt of the Lang farm feeling relieved that it was over, yet guilty about my own actions. It felt like my heart was breaking as my purity had been ripped from my young, innocent soul. But most of all, I felt ashamed. I had put myself in harm's way. I had knowingly done something that would hurt me.

A part of me had wanted to get hurt because my dad's drinking hurt too much, and the pain in my cheek wasn't enough of a distraction. But there was another part of me that truly questioned how bad of a scenario I needed to put myself in before I would find someone to save me. I was seventeen years old and just wanted someone to make me feel safe and taken care of. Deep down, I stupidly believed that if I got myself into a bad enough situation, my dad would sober up and come to my rescue. It was impossible to imagine what it would have taken for me to be brave enough to actually rescue myself.

A large exhalation escaped from my lungs. I glanced up at the stars and caught sight of Orion's Belt, and it took me back to memories of simpler times: nights on the trampoline with my family, stargazing and pointing at shooting stars.

The balmy summer night beat down on me as I slipped off my shoes. I wanted to feel the dirt between my toes. I wanted to feel as grounded as I possibly could in that moment. I didn't want to go home, but I didn't want to stay down on the ground, either. I sat for a little while longer in silence, gazing at the five-hundred-acre cotton field that led to my house. And then I stood up and started walking.

This was one of my first sexual experiences, and from that moment on, I carried the effects of the assault with me. These ranged from depression to panic attacks to PTSD, anxiety, and depression. It wasn't until I met Grant and experienced his calm steadiness that I learned what it meant to be loved. But since I hadn't done the work to recover from my past traumas, that same consistency felt dull and uninspired. I was addicted to the substances my brain created during extreme highs and lows. And like any good addict, I resisted and resented anyone who tried to take my preferred substance away.

In the present day, between the trips and the emotional lows, I was hitting professional highs that I never imagined would come true. rewardStyle had grown over the years, and the company was bringing in over a billion dollars in sales each year. I had continued studying what my readers were buying. I also looked at the back end to see what my readers were buying outside of the things I recommended. For example, when two readers bought the same cute dress from Nordstrom at a friendly price point, I bought it and wrote a post showing my readers how to style it. This led to many more purchases of that same dress.

Over time, I linked to more and more categories so that I was commissioning home decor and beauty products in addition to clothes and accessories. Slowly but surely, this all paid off. When I was named one of rewardStyle's Top 25 Publishers, I felt incredibly proud. It was an accomplishment that spoke to the loyalty of my readers and the (hopefully) positive impact I was having on their lives.

Shortly after, I agreed to do an all-cotton capsule collection for the brand Splendid. This meant that I would design a clothing collection for the brand and put my own name on it. It meant so much to me to continue tying my work to my roots, and I'd always loved Splendid's clean and simple designs. We created staple items from my personal closet, things that people would look at and think, *Oh, that's so Jacey*, including a white cotton shirtdress, basic cotton T-shirts and button-downs, and heather cotton sweatpants.

The collaboration with Splendid was a big deal. I negotiated it myself, and it got a ton of press. It was surreal to see my face on the window of Splendid stores, and it felt good to be focusing on work and meeting my goals.

That year was the biggest New York Fashion Week of my career, thanks to the relationships I'd been forging during all those trips to New York and by supporting their brands year-round. For the first time, I was seated in the front row at every show I attended, and I had at least ten pieces of sponsored content going up each day.

In between each show, I had a photo shoot or an Instagram
Live. Plus, I had to change outfits in between each picture
and show. Brands sent different outfits to all fashion week
attendees, particularly those seated in the front row, and photographers who were there to shoot the show also captured
the audience. If everyone sitting in the front row was wearing a different item from the next season's collection, it was
like a billboard for the brand. It was such a treat to get to
wear these items, but it was a lot of pressure to be wearing
the right thing at the right time with so much going on. I
was getting up at 5:00 a.m. to get my hair and makeup done
and didn't have a moment to breathe throughout the day.

My friend Ashley from E! had just left her job as a fashion segment producer to start her own blog. She had been
attending fashion week as a producer for years, so she was
invited to many of the shows. All week, like any good
friend would do, she was asking to meet up and ride or
walk together to shows. I loved Ashley. She was a dear
friend and had been a bridesmaid in my wedding. But I had
every minute of my days planned out and barely made the
time to respond. I could tell that she was upset. Of course,
I could have welcomed her into the fold and found a way
to make her feel like she belonged, but I told myself there
was nothing I could do. I was working.

In particular, Ashley wanted to walk into the Zimmermann show together. Ever since my Australia trip, I had
been developing a close relationship with the brand, and
they had invited me backstage before the show. I was telling
Ashley this as I was frantically getting dressed in a leopard
dress with black boots and a leather jacket.

"I have to go backstage first, but I'll see you there, okay, Ash?" Haleigh was zipping me up, and my phone sat on a small table in front of us on speaker.

"Okay." I could hear the disappointment in her voice. "Did I tell you I picked up the cutest leopard dress by Zimmermann from Saks to wear?"

Haleigh and I looked at each other. "Ash," I said carefully. "Shoot, is it strapless?" Ashley described the exact dress that I had just put on. "That's the dress they sent *me* to wear," I said. When the brand sent an influencer something to wear to the show, they didn't send it to anyone else. It was all meticulously planned out.

"Well, I don't have anything else to wear," she said with a friendly smile to her voice. "So, I guess we'll just be twinning."

Speaking of twinning, Haleigh and I now had matching pained expressions on our faces. We hung up, and I jumped into damage-control mode. On one hand, not wanting to wear the same outfit as a friend was very stuck-up and immature of me. But on the other hand, this was New York Fashion Week, and I was going to be sitting in the front row. I was being petty and selfish, but in the moment it felt like what I was wearing did truly matter.

Thankfully, Zimmermann had generously sent me two outfits to choose from. The other was a cropped dusty-pink leather bustier-style top with a matching midi-length wrap leather skirt. It was beautiful, but I felt much more confident in the leopard dress. Looking back, I wish I had just worn the darn dress. The world would not have ended if Ashley and I had worn the same thing! But I was too caught up in my ego to realize this at the time and found myself feeling resentful of Ashley, who had done absolutely nothing wrong.

After my visit backstage, I was talking to some other bloggers and photographers near my seat when Ashley found us and joined our conversation. I introduced her around and the lights started to flicker, signaling that the show was about to begin.

"Do you think I can just sit here next to you?" I said nothing, feeling completely torn. I wanted to be a good friend to Ashley, but I was too focused on my precious first-row seat.

I stared straight ahead and tried to focus on the show. I was always floored by Zimmermann's designs, prints, and fabrics, and that season was no exception. Afterward, I was planning to walk out of the show with a few other girls to get our pictures taken by the street-style photographers who would be waiting outside. I cringed, leaving Ashley in the dust, but hoped that maybe she would understand and not feel too hurt.

With so much going on, I was only at home in LA for a few days the rest of that month. On one of those days, I called Ashley. "You were being so mean to me at fashion week," she told me angrily. "You treated me like the scum of the earth. I wouldn't treat my enemies that way."

I snapped back at her, saying, "Maybe we just need to take some space from our friendship." Ashley agreed and we slammed the phone down on each other.

Some small part of me must have known that she was right because I reacted by getting angry. After Ashley hung up, I went inside the house and started noisily getting myself some water, closing the cabinet doors just a little bit too loudly. Grant heard the commotion and came into the kitchen. "What's wrong?"

"Ashley is all upset with me," I told him. "We've been friends for so long, and that's all over now because I apparently dodged her at fashion week."

Grant looked at me. "I mean, that sounds pretty petty, Jacey," he said calmly. "My feelings would probably be hurt, too."

I shook my head and poured a glass of wine and headed back to my office. "Fine, take her side," I said quietly as I passed him. "I'm not surprised."

Of course, Ashley was right. I was being a terrible friend to her and a terrible wife to Grant. But it was easier to blame everyone around me than it was to look in the mirror. It felt less painful to read hateful comments about myself and tell myself that they were true than to actually dig deep to find out why they were so easy for me to believe.

Worst of all, I had become one of the mean girls that I hated most. I was knowingly doing things that not only hurt myself, but that also hurt my friends, my family, and Grant. I knew that something had to change, but I hadn't reached my breaking point yet, so it was easier to hide, to run, and to numb myself by escaping into the perfection of this highly competitive, inauthentic world.

8

Under the Tuscan Sun

AFTER WE SETTLED INTO THE NEW HOUSE, IT WAS clear that Grant and I had to do something to reconnect, or to at least try. On the one hand, I was content living our separate lives with me in New York every other week and him back in Los Angeles doing whatever it was he wanted to do. But on the other hand, I knew deep down that this kind of relationship wasn't healthy. We had drifted so far apart from each other, and all the tension between us still remained unspoken. It sat there heavily, like a cliché of an elephant in the room.

I had been invited to an event in Florence during men's fashion week in the fall, so we decided to fly out early and spend a few days together in Tuscany. Delicious wine, the

beautiful Tuscan countryside, and a few days all to ourselves in a picturesque villa that looked like it was straight
out of the world's most romantic movie. What could go
wrong?

In one word—*everything*. Grant and I hadn't spent any
real time together in so long, and it showed. We were out
of sync with each other in every way, from our sleep sched-
ules to our jet lag to how we wanted to spend our time.
On our first morning, I woke up early as usual to go for
a run. I crept out of the room at 6:30 a.m. so I wouldn't
wake Grant up, but after I'd finished a long run, show-
ered, and gotten dressed, I was ready to start the day, and
Grant was still asleep.

"Come on, wake up," I said, coming out of the bathroom. Grant just moaned and rolled over in bed, so I went
to the windows and opened up the curtains. The room was
flooded with sunlight, and I almost gasped at the stunning
view of the vineyards.

"It's so beautiful!" I told him. "Come on, get up. We're
in Tuscany! Let's go seize the day."

Grant finally got up, and after breakfast we did some
sightseeing and wine tasting, but mostly he just wanted to
relax around the villa. In theory, this sounded lovely, but
I couldn't seem to do it. I was antsy, always wanting to
move and run and GO. Sitting still felt impossible to me.

I told myself (and Grant) that it was my job to stay active even when I was traveling. This wasn't a work trip
per se, but it wasn't *not* a work trip, either. There was no
separation between my life and my work. My readers at
home were following along with me and expected me to

post about what I was doing all day. I felt guilty sleeping in or just relaxing because it didn't provide my readers with any value.

Grant understood that this was my job, but he hadn't traveled with me in so long. He had easily forgotten how all-consuming my work was while I was traveling. In his mind, we were on vacation. He wanted to just relax and enjoy ourselves and work later. The truth is he wasn't wrong, but I wasn't wrong, either. We just hadn't found a way to combine my work with our life together. We hadn't even really tried.

On our last day in Tuscany before moving on to Florence, we decided to visit the Castello Vicchiomaggio, a stone castle that dated back to the 1100s and sat on top of a hill surrounded by gorgeous vineyards. I had booked a guided tour, and I was so excited for a picture-perfect day. That morning, I spent hours on the website scoping out where on the property I could get the best shots, coordinating with the event manager, and planning my outfit, a Chloe top with black shorts and my Aquazzura black strappy ballet flats.

This was how I ran the blog back then. Over time, the blog had gravitated away from photos I had snapped of myself in the parking lot to showcasing more and more high-end designer items in editorialized images. Everything was perfectly coordinated and styled, from the location and wardrobe to hair and makeup and accessories, just like a photo spread in a magazine.

With so many bloggers and influencers out there at this point, posting high-end designer labels legitimized the blog because it meant those brands were choosing to work with me. I couldn't deny the fact that my readers responded to these images, too. As I moved in this direction, each photo I posted started getting fifty comments or more, which had never happened before. More engagement equaled more success. When brands saw that my photos featuring their products were receiving ten thousand likes on Instagram with hundreds of comments, it was a win for them and a win for me.

Yes, I was giving my readers what they wanted, but I was also hiding behind these glossy, highly stylized images. I noticed that when I posted them, it didn't lead to as many nasty comments on *The Forum* questioning what was going on in my life or my marriage. To preempt these questions, whenever I did post about more personal things, I manipulated it so that it would seem like Grant and I were on solid ground. If a hotel left me flowers or I bought myself something, I posted a picture saying they were from *someone special*. When I got back to LA after a trip, I made a big dinner, set the table beautifully, and posted about how nice it was to come back to a home-cooked meal. Then I struck the table, took the food into the living room, and ate in front of the TV alone.

Clearly, none of us should believe what we see on social media. Yet to this day there is still so much pressure to keep up and maintain a lifestyle that looks good in photos. This leads to FOMO and a tendency to measure our lives against other people's. Add any type of mental health issue or a job that requires posting about your life online, and it's a very slippery slope toward crippling insecurity and depression. I tumbled down this hill willingly, telling myself that it was my job and I had no choice but to organize every moment of my life around an online facade.

It was my intention to create such a facade on the trip to Castello Vicchiomaggio. Everything had to be perfect. To get there, we were relying on the old-school GPS that came with our Italian rental car and a printed-out map. This would have been a test for any marriage. I was anxious during the whole ride and acting like the ultimate back-seat driver, and Grant's calm and cool demeanor quickly faded in the Tuscan sun.

"Dammit," Grant said, banging his hand against the steering wheel once he finally admitted that we were lost. We had pulled over underneath an ancient bridge while threatening clouds started to loom overhead.

"I told you to make a left back at that farm-looking place," I snapped, staring at the unfolded map in my lap.

"Well, this street is one-way," Grant said with frustration. "I have no idea how to get us back there."

"Great," I said, tossing the map aside. "There go the pictures I needed to get today."

Grant turned in his seat to face me. "That's really all you care about, isn't it?" he yelled. I sat there, somewhat in shock. I don't think I had ever heard Grant raise his voice before. "I'm so sick of this. You're always gone, and I don't want to live my entire life like it's one big photo shoot. This is not what I signed up for."

Just then, the skies opened and enormous pieces of hail the size of golf balls started thundering down. While I thought I had experienced every type of weather imaginable in South Texas, I had never seen anything like this before. The hail was the perfect backdrop to our fight. I had to raise my voice to be heard over the deafening clamor, but of course, I probably would have been yelling anyway. I had so much anger and resentment toward Grant built up inside of me at that point. I had made the argument against him over and over in my head, refining it more and more each time like I was polishing a stone. Now I unleashed it all as I told Grant about the many ways he'd let me down and abandoned me.

Once it was all out, we just sat there in silence, waiting for the storm to pass. I was breathing heavily and could feel adrenaline coursing through my body. I wanted to open the car door and run away. Instead, I took a few deep breaths and forced my mind to think about our next stop, Florence, and plan a shot list in my head.

Yes, Grant had just told me that he was tired of his life being one big photo shoot, and there I was, planning out my very next photos. We'd both laid it all on the table, but honestly, I simply wasn't ready to change. I was also in complete denial about the fact that my marriage was falling apart and that it wasn't Grant's fault alone. I have since gained the courage and self-awareness to know better. I was letting Grant down every day by leaving him both emotionally and physically.

Of course, I was aware at the time that Grant and I were having problems, and had been for a while, but it seemed impossible to withstand the true weight of those problems. So, I stuffed them down and continued to focus on my work, my perfectionism, and *my* life. I was so selfish and self-absorbed that I couldn't, and wouldn't, stop for two minutes to look at the ways I was contributing to *our* problems.

The next day, we arrived in Florence. Grant had studied abroad in Florence when he was in college, and it is a hub of European fashion, so it's a city we each loved for very different reasons. I had been invited to the closing party of a weekend-long event thrown by Luisa Via Roma, a high-end European retailer. They invited the top influencers from around the world for an over-the-top experience they called FIRENZE4EVER. For three days, attendees created their own looks from the most coveted brands in the world. Max Mara, Versace, Balmain, and Alexander Wang were only a few of the dozens of high-end, luxury fashion labels that were associated with Luisa Via Roma. It had been one of my goals for a while to be included in this event. For the first time that year, I was invited to the blowout party at the end of the weekend, which I saw as my first step toward a future invitation to the whole shebang.

On our first night in Florence, Grant and I checked into The Westin Excelsior, a stunning hotel with Renaissance-style decor and views of the Arno River. We unpacked, had a quiet dinner, and then got into bed. In the dark, I stared up at the ceiling. I could tell that Grant was awake beside me, but for a long time, neither of us spoke. Finally, I broke the silence.

"We're not happy," I said simply.

It was a statement, not a question, but I realized that I was holding my breath, waiting for Grant's reply. After what seemed like a long time, he just said, "Yeah." It was a relief, but at the same time, it was terrifying to hear him voice the feelings I had been harboring for so long. Deep down, of course I had known we weren't happy, but there was something about saying it out loud that made it real.

For so long, I'd been running from anything real. Online, I'd been pretending that everything with Grant was fine, that he was sending me flowers and we were sharing cozy homemade meals. I'd shared beautiful pictures of us wine tasting on our miserable trip to Tuscany. I posted cheerful replies to comments when I was really feeling like crap. The only thing that was real were those few words we said to each other in the dark.

"I want you to be a part of my life," I told Grant. "I feel so abandoned. No one even knows we're married. I just wish you were a part of it—the trips, my work, everything."

Grant sighed. "I want to be a part of your life, too," he said. "But I don't want to be on display. I don't want to be *Mr. Damsel.* It makes me feel like an idiot."

"I know," I told him. "I get it. I don't want to make you do something you don't want to do."

And that was it. Nothing was settled, nothing was fixed, but it felt like the air had cleared a little. Grant and I hadn't been talking to each other much, and certainly not about how we really felt. In a strange way, voicing our unhappiness made us feel more connected than we had been in a long time.

I woke up the next morning feeling hopeful that Grant had really heard me and would make more of an effort to be engaged. But had I really heard him? Yes and no. I understood where he was coming from when he said that he didn't want to be known as *Mr. Damsel*, but at the same time, I didn't know how I could sustain my work without having him be a part of it.

It felt like I had to choose between Grant and my work, and I didn't want to do that. Through my actions, I had been choosing my work, but it was much harder to voice that choice out loud or even admit it to myself. For the first time, I honestly questioned what I really wanted. It was the right question and one I should have asked myself much sooner, but I didn't have an answer.

The theme of Luisa Via Roma that year was blue (fitting for my mood). For the finale party, I wore a short IRO Paris cocktail dress that was bright blue and paired it with a statement necklace by DYLANLEX and a nautical striped Chanel clutch. Grant wore a beautiful navy blue suit that we purchased just for the occasion. When I came out of the bathroom after getting ready and saw Grant in his suit, I felt those butterflies in my stomach like when we'd first met.

LA is such a casual city, and Grant was an LA boy through and through. He almost always wore jeans and black or gray T-shirts with cool hats and sneakers. Obviously, there's nothing wrong with that, but seeing him all dolled up was a refreshing change.

"You look cute," I told Grant as he popped a bottle of champagne. We smiled at each other, feeling a spark of much-needed hope as our glasses clinked together.

Luisa Via Roma had rented out a huge cathedral for

the party. It was dark inside and packed with people, with champagne fountains flowing and a whole world of fashion that didn't exist in the United States. The guests, outfits, and atmosphere felt very different from any event I'd been to back home. It was my first time at this event, and I barely knew anyone there, so Grant and I were both experiencing it anew together. We stood to the side and watched the international crowd, all decked out in the season's latest styles. When I recognized someone, I whispered who they were in Grant's ear. It felt good to be on the sidelines, taking it all in together like a cohesive unit, a team.

After the party, we walked back to the hotel and had a late dinner with more champagne. I hadn't hired a photographer, so we didn't take any pictures. The only photo I was able to capture was taken by the concierge at our hotel. It showed Grant and me standing side by side but far apart, holding hands and looking at each other. It felt very symbolic of our union at that time. We had hope. We loved each other. Yet we were still very far apart.

Back in LA, we quickly fell back into our old patterns. I had a ton of travel already booked for the weeks immediately following Luisa Via Roma. I partnered with *Travel + Leisure* and Cathay Pacific Airways on a trip to Hong Kong, a bucket-list goal for me, and then traveled to Dubai for the first time to speak at SIMPLY, an international fashion and beauty conference. These were huge career milestones. It felt like I had hit my professional peak, but I kept pushing harder, chasing the dragon, because I was so desperate to feel something different, something more.

I sat in my first-class seat to Hong Kong, thinking, *This*

is a huge moment. Why am I feeling so lonely? I had an idea in my mind of what living an accomplished and successful life would feel like. But there wasn't any amount of clothes or first-class seats that would actually make me feel loved. No matter what I did, I was still left feeling a void within me. I was completely unfulfilled, but I had no idea how to fill that void with anything other than superficiality, perfectionism, and achievements.

I desperately wanted something to shake me out of my paralyzed state, but I would not have wished for the thing that finally happened. Every time I returned home from a trip, I would drop my bags and embrace my old bulldog, William. William was getting older and had started having seizures. Every time I left for another trip, I worried that something would happen to William while I was gone.

One morning, Grant was at work and I was home alone, a rarity, when William started having another seizure. I ran to him and knelt on the kitchen floor and began doing chest compressions the way the vet had shown me in case this happened. After a few minutes, I knew it wasn't working. William was still unconscious.

I sat back on my heels and quickly surveyed the situation. I had to get William to the vet right away. There was no one around to help me, and he weighed about seventy pounds. But I couldn't waste any time. My emotions were bouncing between feeling stable and in control and having a full-blown meltdown as I awkwardly scooped William up in my arms and braced myself to stand. I could barely do it. He was so heavy and unwieldy. I had to take what felt like a hundred breaks to get from the kitchen to the car as

I staggered my way one step at a time, but I finally made it. As I reached the car, William was still unconscious and tears were streaming down my face.

At the vet's, they resuscitated William and began running tests. I was hysterical, but tried to remain calm. At least he was still alive, I told myself. Maybe he was going to be okay. They referred us to a heart specialist, and we made an appointment for the next day, which happened to be the day of a huge shoot I was doing for Bloomingdale's. We were shooting at multiple locations, and it was a major production: a hair and makeup team, stylists, a lighting team, photographers, and so on. It was a big deal, and I had been working on it with the team at Bloomingdale's for months.

When we got William home and snuggled into his bed, I curled up against him, spooning him. Before I went to sleep, I whispered in his ear, "It's okay, Willie. If you need to go, I will be okay."

The next morning, I woke up at 5:00 a.m. and spent some time giving William kisses in his little dog bed before leaving for the all-day shoot. Grant was planning to take William to the doctor while I was gone. I met the Bloomingdale's production team at the Avalon Hotel, where we had held fittings a few days before. I spent two hours in the hair and makeup chair before the entire team of eight loaded up in the sprinter van. Over the next several hours, we shot about a dozen different looks in about a dozen different locations around Los Angeles.

We were finally at our last location when Grant called me. "I'm so sorry—I have to take this," I told the team, and quickly answered the phone. "Is he okay?" There was a pause, and in that moment I knew.

"He had a heart attack, and died on the table." Grant was crying. Grant never cried.

My entire body started shaking as I burst out in tears. "What? What do you mean? Where are you?" My voice began to rise and sound hysterical.

"I'm driving to get you. Where are you?" Grant said, weeping.

There I was, at Paper or Plastik Cafe, with tears ruining the makeup that had been expertly applied and touched up throughout the day. My beloved William, who had been with me for eleven years and seen me through so many ups and downs, was gone. For a moment, it felt like I floated out of my body and was looking down at myself. And I realized that I had actually been floating for years. The trips, the clothes, the competition. All of a sudden, the bubble burst and I landed with a thud.

William's death, while traumatic in and of itself, was the straw that broke the camel's back of my fake, filtered life. It opened my eyes to another loss I had been experiencing for years—the slow and painful crumbling of my marriage and my entire sense of self. I had unintentionally been avoiding tuning in to myself and putting in the time and care that my marriage needed and deserved. If the relationship between me and Grant was a bank account, I had been taking withdrawal after withdrawal: the trips, the avoidance, the denial, the way I put my heart into my work. The account was nearly empty at this point, and

William's death was the final withdrawal that our relationship could take.

After rushing to the hospital and saying one final goodbye to William, we returned home. I could tell by our other bulldog Polly's sullen demeanor and neediness that she was feeling just as bereft without her buddy as Grant and I were. It hit me that William's loss would shift the dynamic of our home in so many different ways. For now, I cuddled up with Polly and cried and cried, for once letting myself fully feel the emotions that threatened to overwhelm me.

It may sound silly, but the following day I was worried about how to announce William's death to my followers. It felt so raw, and I didn't know how they would react. The last things I wanted to deal with were questions, judgments, or criticism. But after twenty-four hours, I felt ready, and I knew that writing about William would be therapeutic, regardless of the response. So, I wrote from my heart about how much William had meant to our family and the pain we were in, and I shared it in a post with about a dozen photos of William and me together throughout the years.

I had posted personal things before, but nothing this intimate, and certainly not in a long time. I braced myself for the response. Grant and I lay in bed that afternoon with Polly and watched old reruns of *Friends*. I didn't open my phone for a few hours. When I did, I saw that my post about William had received hundreds of comments from followers, all expressing their condolences and sharing stories and pics of their own beloved pets. I drew so much comfort from reading them and realized that others who had gone through a loss might be drawing comfort from my words, too.

Then the flowers started to arrive, dozens and dozens and dozens of flowers. We had so many flowers that we had nowhere to put all of them. It was such an incredible outpouring of love, and I was able to fully see the magnitude of the community I had created. It was overwhelming.

For about a week, Grant and I mourned together. We cried and napped and reminisced about our William. We barely worked or even left the house. On some level, we both knew that we were mourning more than just William. This was the beginning of what was going to be a difficult time in our lives.

Despite the loss and the ways in which we came together to grieve, things were still not right between us. We were both sad, but we weren't angry. It was simply time to face the truth that things between us weren't working.

At the end of that month, without any fighting or drama or an instigating event, Grant and I started to talk about separating. I was the one who originally brought it up, but I was heartbroken when Grant agreed. To me, this confirmed that things really were fundamentally wrong between us. I thought that if we were meant to stay together, Grant would want to stay and fight for us. But by then I had to face the fact that I had been the one who was running. I was just as much, if not more, to blame for the gulf between us as he was.

The conversation took place over several painful, tearful weeks as we debated what to do. Our talks felt very heavy yet matter-of-fact as we discussed how we should tell our parents that we were separating and if and when I should share the news with my followers. At times, we jumped three steps ahead and talked about how it would feel if we each dated other people. We talked about the big *D* word. Then we jumped three steps back and reminisced about how happily engaged we once were, both of us dissolving into tears.

How had we gotten from there to here? It seemed impossible, and more than anything, I wanted to rewind the tape and do things better from the start. That feeling of regret was the most painful one of all. It was the emotion I'd been running from for years.

Yet, for the first time in a very long time, it felt strangely comforting to be able to talk to Grant in such an unfiltered way. I wished it hadn't taken us so long to finally talk openly about our relationship. But I finally accepted the fact that at least half of the blame lay with me. I needed to clean up my side of the street, because it was messier than Grant's. And not just because of what I hadn't put into our marriage, but also because of how I had been failing myself.

I had become very good at living a fake life and bad at living my real one. Now I had to fix what was broken within me before Grant and I had a chance of making things work, before I had a chance of feeling happiness and fulfillment on any level. I needed space to clear my mind, to feel what it was like to be completely alone, and to figure out what I really wanted.

I met Grant when I was twenty-five years old, got married when I was twenty-eight, and here I was at nearly thirty-three with zero idea of what I really wanted in life.

Of course, I knew I wanted all the things that everyone thinks they want: a happy marriage, a happy home, and a successful career. But what did any of that really mean? The truth is I had no idea.

Until that point, I hadn't been willing to even consider what it might take to create my own happiness. I had been too busy running from the people who cared about me out of my own deep fear of abandonment. I wasn't aware of it, but the scared little girl inside of me knew that if she ran first, no one else could leave her. That's why I ran from Grant, was such a jerk to friends like Ashley, and put all my energy into a career that I knew could never abandon me, or ever love me back.

Only a small handful of our friends knew what was going on between me and Grant. The last thing I wanted was for my followers to find out the truth. I didn't want them to see how imperfect my life really was beyond the sheen of social media or how much I had failed. I had already let myself down so much. I had already let Grant down so much. I didn't want to let them down, too. And letting all my dirty laundry out to dry for the entire world to see and judge wasn't going to do anyone any good.

At the end of the day, I needed to learn how to set boundaries for myself and my family on social media, as well as with the people I surrounded myself with. Just as I had learned how to set boundaries around what I would allow in, I also needed to carefully consider what I was putting back out into the world. I had been continuously making bad choices, lying to myself and to others, and hurting people along the way. I had hurt Grant, too, in the deepest way possible. It didn't seem necessary to share these failings with my readers, and I felt that by revealing every single crack in my marriage, it would only make things harder for Grant and me to ever stand a chance at recovering, whether that was together or apart. So, I continued posting beautiful pictures of beautiful things.

Once we had made the decision to separate, Grant rented an Airbnb in Venice Beach and moved out. Even though I had been the one pushing for it, I was shocked. Grant was my rock, and just like that, he was gone. I tried to keep in touch with him, assuming that we'd stay connected for however long we were separated, but Grant was firm.

"We can check in with each other briefly once a day," he told me, "but we're separated now. You wanted time, and I'm giving you time."

And that was it. For the first time in my life, I was left alone with no distractions, nowhere to run, no one else to blame for my unhappiness but me. It was time—past time, really—to look deep inside at the broken pieces I had been avoiding for so long, and finally do the work that was needed to heal them.

9

Rebranding

WHILE GRANT AND I WERE SEPARATED, I DIDN'T travel, and for the first time in a long time, I felt truly alone. I was still working, but I took it slow and stayed home by myself. I didn't go to events. I didn't bounce around town and try to distract myself. My mind felt so clouded, and I needed space to unravel what had happened and how I had gotten here.

I knew that I loved Grant, that he loved me, and that we wanted to be together. Those things were clear. But I also felt so strongly that something was fundamentally broken. Was it actually a problem between us, or a problem within me?

I took a hard, long look at myself, which immediately

propelled me into a state of discomfort. This forced me to step outside of myself, outside of my rut, and away from all the tiny voices in my head. I observed my thoughts. My reactions. My triggers. And it was painfully clear that in some essential way, I was incomplete. I had never truly faced my childhood or healed from it. I had kept moving forward blindly, leaving many pieces of myself untied. It was time to wrap them up, not necessarily in a pretty bow, but in a way that left me complete and whole.

I dived into the project of healing myself with single-minded dedication. I read all the books and did all the meditation and all the yoga. I started a fresh new journal, and each morning I wrote down inspiring quotes I found online or in books, along with a list of everything I was grateful for that day. This helped me stay in a positive mindset. The books that helped me the most were *When Things Fall Apart*, *The Clarity Cleanse*, and *The Miracle Morning*.

These books taught me to practice sitting still and observing my thoughts without truly identifying with them as a label of who I was as a person. When I was on the back porch sipping coffee or taking a walk around the block, I paused and looked at every thought that entered my mind rather than immediately identifying with that thought and taking action to defend it.

For many years, it had been so easy to "Report Spam" on an erroneous message that infiltrated my inbox, but it was much more difficult to do this with intrusive thoughts that flooded my mind. I dedicated all my efforts toward observing my thoughts and my mental states. When I felt insecure, I thought about what had triggered that feeling instead of jumping online to post a filtered pic and make myself feel better. When I felt extreme sadness overwhelm me, I asked myself what was making me feel sad instead of doing something impulsive and misguided that I thought might make me happy.

My goal was to look at my thoughts and emotions as objectively as possible. This is a classic mindfulness technique, and I worked extremely hard to teach myself that I was not defined by every thought or feeling that came in my direction. It was a struggle!

For years leading up to this point, I was so disconnected from my true identity that I had been attaching to every intrusive thought that popped into my brain about who I was as a person. I believed my nasty inner voice when it told me that I had to work harder than anyone else and be perfect in order to be loved, and that it was okay to resent other people for not being perfect or not trying as hard as me.

Disconnecting from that voice allowed me to see myself as I truly was. At my core, I was not a mean person. I also didn't really love being in the spotlight or being in control 24/7. And I certainly didn't ever want to make other people feel bad about themselves. My rudeness over the past couple of years was merely an imitation of strength to mask the fact that I felt very weak. And my behavior had been in complete misalignment with my true self.

So, who was I? I was someone who loved gardening, playing the piano, and being creative. I was the type of person who wanted everyone in the room to feel loved.

I was someone who woke up every day with curiosity, a good sense of humor, and a lighthearted outlook. And I was imperfect. My nails were still always bitten and my hair never laid exactly right. But maybe—*maybe*—that was okay, and maybe that meant it was okay for other people to be imperfect, too.

Ironically, I realized that I craved unconditional love and stability more than anything. But my intrusive thoughts of not being good enough and my fears of being abandoned led me to bolt in the opposite direction, running myself ragged and destroying my marriage in the process. The whole time I craved the security of Grant and home. Yet I ran from those exact things that I wanted most. I was like a designer with no identity taking wild swings of the pendulum with their style. But the best designers and the people who are most true to themselves allow the different parts of themselves to flow into each other, enhancing and informing the total package.

I had started going to therapy for about six months before the separation, but my therapist and I had never delved deeply into my childhood. I went into my next session and asked, "What is wrong with me?" My therapist explained that my childhood trauma was still determining how I reacted to stress in the present day. I had been in a state of survival, or fight or flight, for my entire childhood. This made it impossible for me to sit still with stressful emotions, and it led me to experience fighting and drama as love. Without this chaos, Grant's steadiness felt like a lack of connection because my nervous system wasn't triggered the way it was used to being around people who loved me.

My family's coping mechanism to deal with the stress of my dad's drinking and my parents' fighting was to put on a facade every time we left the house and present ourselves to the outside world as the perfect family. We essentially lived a double life. This is typical in families that struggle with addiction.

In a way, the children of alcoholics are basically born to be influencers. We are experts at making everything look beautiful and perfect to mask the ugly truth. This skill had certainly contributed to my success, but I realized now that it was also keeping me stuck in an unhealthy cycle of seeking chaos and reactivity behind the scenes and glossing it over with a shiny public veneer. This was my own addiction, and it was keeping me stuck in a physiological state of fear and stress. To be healthy and "sober" myself, I had to break this cycle.

To do so, my therapist and I began EMDR therapy, which means eye movement desensitization and reprocessing. I know this sounds "out there," but it completely changed the way I reacted to emotional stress. It basically works by removing the physiological stress response associated with traumatic memories. By going back to the memory in your mind in great detail and finding a resolution while simultaneously triggering certain parts of the brain, you effectively rewire the way your body and mind react to those memories.

In my therapist's office, I went back to some of my most painful memories. It occurred to me now that the earliest ones all had to do with my parents leaving me. I'd had terrible separation anxiety and hated when they left Justin and me, though it happened rarely.

I recalled one incident when they had to leave town for a funeral, and I stood in the driveway, screaming and crying hysterically, begging them not to go. When they started pulling away, I chased them down the driveway until my little legs couldn't keep up with their station wagon. I fell to my knees in the gravel driveway with tears and snot pouring down my face.

Sitting in my therapist's office in a meditative state with electrodes attached to my forehead, I could *feel* the pain of my parents leaving me, and I broke down sobbing as my therapist instructed me to reassure little Jacey and tell her that it was going to be okay. It was gut-wrenching work. I showed up to a meeting after therapy with major raccoon eyes from crying off my mascara. But it felt like I'd reprocessed a little piece of pain. I was ready to accept full responsibility for changing myself.

It was a start. My fear of my parents' abandonment ran deeper, though, so we continued revisiting moments when I felt it the most strongly. Shortly after they returned from that funeral, when I was in sixth grade, I developed an intense fear of going to school. Every morning began normally, but as my mom's car slowly approached my school, my anxiety levels started to rise. The developing fear intensified as she fought against me, and just as we pulled up to school, I begged my mom to turn around and go back home.

After being absent for nearly two weeks, I woke up one morning with high spirits, hoping to power through and get myself to school. I dressed in a yellow floral sleeveless blouse and matching yellow floral shorts with white oxfords. But as the car drove farther and farther away from our house, the familiar sinking feeling in the pit of my stomach began to form.

Sensing the shift in my attitude, my mom threatened, "If you don't make it today, your dad is gonna give you the belt."

At that point, I would have gladly accepted the belt over the torture of being dropped off at school. It's not that I didn't *want* to go to school. I just couldn't. I was completely immobilized by fear. The closer to school our Suburban inched, the heavier and deeper that pit in my stomach sank. The car pulled into the parking lot, and my hands gripped firmly on the inside door handle. Tears streamed down my cheeks as I pleaded with my mom.

"Please, Mom, please don't make me go," I begged her.

"That's it!" my mom snapped. "I'm callin' your dad and *he* can figure out what to do with you."

A few minutes later, my mom stood in the front driveway, holding on to my left arm as my dad's black truck turned wildly down our tiny farm road. The man who stepped out of the truck was not the same person I had shared beers with on our secret fishing trip. His face was pale, his eyes sunken. He looked tired, frustrated, and filled with rage. But I didn't believe he would do it. Deep down, I did not believe he would do it.

My dad had spanked Justin and me a few times in the past, but it was always half-hearted. My dad never truly seemed angry with us, and we nearly chuckled through them, knowing that he was just going through the motions. This time was different. My dad grabbed my right arm, dragging me over to the side yard as my entire body weight fought against him.

"Dad! No!"

His firm grip turned my tiny frame to face the field, and I heard him whip his belt outside of the loops.

He knelt down, bending me over one of his knees. The belt hurt so much that halfway through my beating there was urine streaming down my legs, ruining my new favorite yellow shorts. The grip of his hand on my other arm hurt almost as much.

"I'm sorry," I cried, feeling deep down that I deserved this.

My dad fought to catch his breath as he retrieved his belt.

"Go to your room," he ordered.

"What do you want to say to that Jacey?" My therapist's voice shook me back into the present moment. But in my mind, I was still back there. Both little Jacey and adult Jacey were crying, feeling hurt and abandoned and completely, utterly unlovable and alone. I was crying so hard that I could barely speak. "What do you want to tell her?" she nudged kindly.

"It's okay," I whispered to myself through my tears. "It's going to be okay. You didn't deserve that."

I dreaded going to therapy. It was exhausting and incredibly painful. But the more I went, the more clarity I gained, and the better I eventually started to feel. I was learning that for years this fear of abandonment had superseded everything else in my life. In order to protect myself and avoid that horrible feeling of being abandoned, I made sure to always run away first.

I had sabotaged my relationship with Grant because I was so scared of him leaving me.

This wasn't just the result of a physical abandonment, like my parents going on a trip or dropping me off at school. All parents do things like that. And I'm not here to cry poor me, either. We all experience traumas to some extent. Mine were no greater or worse than anyone else's. I am tremendously grateful for my life and all the privileges I've had. But it was still a lot of work to heal from the ways I had been emotionally neglected by my parents.

My dad was never able to be there for me when he was drinking, and I lived in a state of fear about when he would pick that bottle back up again. Having an unreliable parent leads to a state of constant stress. It changes the way your brain is wired. And my mom was unable to fully be there for me, either. She tried to be both a mother and a father for Justin and me, but she had her own issues and was focused on trying to survive.

I worked through memories of begging my dad not to drink, of some of the worst fights between my parents, my dad lighting the lawn mower on fire in a drunken rage. Memory after memory after memory of the day-to-day pain of living with a dad who was drinking and parents who were fighting 24/7/365. Well, at least the memories that I could remember at all. Peeling back the layers of my past sometimes felt like looking for a needle in a haystack. Because of my PTSD, I have huge gaps in my memory. There have been times when I've seen someone I had known for twenty years or more, yet had zero memory of who they were and how we knew each other.

Ironically, I felt the pain so much more deeply when revisiting my memories now. At the time that it was all happening, I didn't really feel it. I wasn't even aware of how hard things were in the moment because I was so busy trying to hold myself together by putting Band-Aids on my wounds. Now I was going back and peeling all those Band-Aids off. It hurt like hell, but it was the only way I had a chance of really healing. With practice, I learned that I could breathe through those hard moments, feel the pain, and survive. And if I could breathe through one of those hard moments, I could breathe through nearly anything.

As I was working through these issues with my therapist, I was speaking to and addressing them with my dad every day. While my parents did not know that Grant and I were taking some time apart, my dad did know that I was on a path of self-healing, and he was incredibly present and supportive. He deeply regretted the incident with the belt, and still does. But by this point, our relationship had fully healed and we had grown closer than ever. Our relationship wouldn't have been what it was (and still is) if we hadn't gone through all the harder moments, and I wouldn't trade that for anything in the world.

While I was doing this work, it felt very strange to not be sharing the truth of what was going on in my life with my followers. I worried that someone would see through the facade or find out that Grant and I had separated and "out" us. I wanted to be honest with my followers, but I was also learning that my relationship with my work was very unhealthy. Post, post, post, post, post, and share about my life. That was what I had done for years, and as a result, it was what others expected of me. If I had a thought, people expected me to share it. If I ate a burger, they wanted to see the picture. And if something salacious was going on in my life, my readers felt that they deserved to know.

Of course, I didn't blame them for this. They had merely come to expect what I had always given them. But I knew I had to start putting up some boundaries between myself and my work.

First, I started avoiding *The Forum*, especially when I was already feeling down. I scheduled time to check it when I was feeling strong and clear-minded in case there was any useful information on there. This way, it became just another part of my business.

When I did see hurtful comments, I thought about the other person sitting in their house, typing out that bullying message. I imagined how much that stranger must have been hurting if they were choosing to lash out at someone online. Finding compassion for these people took the nasty sting out of even the ugliest comments. And over time, removing that sting helped me to stop being so reliant on the opinions of others to formulate my opinion of myself.

I also took control over who could call and text me so I had more of a separation between my work and my life. I asked publicists and assistants and other people I worked with to rely on email to communicate with me so their energy wasn't affecting me throughout the day. With this boundary in place, I could focus and be present, and my personal life felt a little more sacred without being constantly interrupted with work messages.

These small changes added up, and I started to feel much steadier and less reactive in my day-to-day activities. I also weeded several people out of my life during this time. This wasn't because I didn't love and value their friendships, but I knew they weren't the types of relationships that I could sustain if I wanted to move forward feeling strong and in control. At the same time, Ashley and I got in touch and went to lunch. She apologized, and I also apologized for my behavior at fashion week. She graciously accepted and we've been close friends again ever since.

I hadn't actually changed much yet, but my mask had fallen off, and I was standing in front of the mirror truly looking at myself. Without the mask and the carefully curated outfits and posts, who was I? Outside of therapy and work, I was relearning myself. I stopped running, literally and physically. Instead of forcing myself to get up at 5:00 a.m. to go for a run, I listened to my body's natural rhythms and let myself wake up naturally. I found myself replacing the silky La Perla pajamas that seemed so nice and sexy but made me sweat at night with comfy cotton leggings from Uniqlo and long-sleeved T-shirts by Velvet. I went to the grocery store and bought the foods my body craved instead of what would look good on Instagram. I read the books and went to the museums I was interested in versus the trendier ones.

I experienced what it was like to live a normal life by myself. I had always fought against the grain of feeling like a "normal" person who didn't fly around the world with a closet full of Dior and handpicked pink peonies at the Four Seasons. It wasn't that I thought having a nine-to-five job, going to the grocery store, and making plans for the weekend because you knew you were going to be there wasn't good enough. It was that I thought I wasn't good enough if I lived this type of normal life. I always felt like I should have been doing more, trying harder, and traveling to newer and more exotic places to prove that I was worthy.

What I didn't realize all along was that I was missing the life that was slipping right through my fingers with all that running. As soon as I forced myself to be present in my day-to-day life and reflect on what I had been running away from, it became clear to me that normal was good. Normal was great. But I didn't want a normal life alone. I wanted a best friend who I could stay up with every night talking about life, who I could share the most mundane details of the day with, and who would make them feel like the most important details. And that person was Grant.

I never forgot my mistakes, but I will always remember the lesson.

My therapist suggested that Grant and I go to see a marriage counselor named Stan Meyer, who was apparently famous for being able to tell couples within an hour whether or not their relationship was going to make it. A very small part of me feared that he would tell us to run for the hills, our marriage is doomed. But at least then I would have a black-and-white answer.

Appointments with Dr. Meyer were outrageously expensive and required a two-hour drive to Calabasas, but

Grant and I both wanted to get this right. Only a month into our separation, I felt like I was ready for Grant to move back in, but he kept telling me, "I don't want to do this again. We have to stay the course."

Before our appointment, we filled out tons of paperwork with every detail about ourselves and our marriage. Finally, it was our turn to hear the verdict as to whether or not our marriage was ready for the long haul.

Dr. Meyer walked in twenty minutes late. He started by asking, "How long have you guys been married?"

Are you kidding me? I thought. *This was the renowned therapist?* I bit my tongue and answered his question.

He just nodded. "Have you read my books?"

Seriously? I thought.

"No," Grant and I replied honestly.

"Well, that's a shame," Dr. Meyer said, sounding offended. "If you had read them, you'd already have the foundation and we could have picked up from there. It'll cost us a lot of time having to start from scratch."

I almost lost it on him. But instead, I crossed my arms and shook my foot anxiously, feeling defensive. I wasn't sure if it was a technique or what, but Dr. Meyer noticed right away.

"Why are you tapping your foot?" he asked me. He was so in-your-face and aggressive, and I got a bad vibe from him right away. But we stuck it out and spent the hour breaking down our problems: my anger that Grant wouldn't travel with me or be more involved in my work, his resentment of me for being gone so much and pressuring him to become a blogger husband, and the distance that had grown between us as a result. I shared some of the work I'd been doing in therapy, my abandonment issues, and how hard it had been to feel abandoned by Grant for the past few years.

Dr. Meyer just looked at us. "I don't understand," he said. "You guys are a great couple. You love each other. You respect each other." He turned to me. "So, your dad was an alcoholic. Get over it. Grant is a great guy. What's the problem?"

I stared at him in disbelief. *What an asshole.*

"The problem," I said, "is that I feel like Grant doesn't want to be a part of my world."

"Grant!" Dr. Meyer turned to face him. "Do you want to be a part of her world?"

"Yes," Grant said.

"Well, there you go." Dr. Meyer said, standing up to show us out the door. "You two have a great relationship. Go on a date before our next appointment, and I'll see you next week."

I fumed the entire drive home. I felt like Dr. Meyer had blamed me for all our problems while completely diminishing my own concerns. Grant, of course, felt like a million bucks.

"That went great," he said with a giant smile as we sat in bumper-to-bumper traffic.

I rolled my eyes. "Of course you think so," I said. "He thinks you're God's gift and everything is my fault."

Grant turned to me. "Maybe you should start listening to the experts," he said with a glint in his eye. I couldn't help but smile. As annoyed as I was, it did feel good to hear Dr. Meyer say that he believed in Grant and me as a couple. I had lost hope and could feel Dr. Meyer's faith in us strengthening my resolve.

Later that week, I went to Grant's Airbnb for our date. He cooked me his famous Chicken Thai Pasta and wore an ironed navy blue shirt. I could tell that he had cleaned up not only himself, but also the tiny cottage. There was a tea-light candle at the small table for two, along with some daisies he'd clearly picked up from the Gelson's Market down the street.

I was wearing a white silk tank top with skinny jeans, a tan blazer over my shoulder, and had figured flats were appropriate for the occasion. I had to laugh at how much stress I had put into planning my outfit. At the end of the night, I felt so homesick, even though I was returning to our house. But I wasn't homesick for a house or a place. I was homesick for Grant. We said goodbye and kissed, held each other, and kissed again. I could tell that he wanted more, yet he still asked me to leave, which left me pining.

Our next session with Dr. Meyer was a complete one-eighty from the first. It was as if his intention was to break me down on week one, and now it was Grant's turn. He focused on Grant's family history and coping mechanisms, and it was incredibly eye-opening to watch a therapist uncover why Grant reacted to things the way he did. While my family was always up in each other's faces, Grant's barely communicated. Dr. Meyer explained that he learned to cope by burying his head in the sand and making jokes to defuse awkward situations.

"You've been neglecting your wife," he told Grant. "You

need to pay attention to her. And you both need to start choosing your marriage over everything else in your lives." He told us to pursue each other on a daily basis, from the smallest ways, like always greeting each other and saying goodbye when we came and went throughout the day, to the biggest ways, like taking the idea of separation or divorce off the table completely for at least six months.

"You guys are a great match," he told us, "but you're in your heads, and you're putting too much pressure on yourselves. Just go and have fun together, even if you don't want to. Start going through the motions and your hearts will catch up."

A true commitment to something or someone is a choice that you keep making again and again and again. I know it sounds overly simplistic, but the instruction to just choose each other every day over everything else became our ethos moving forward. That meant I had to choose Grant over my work, too. I never wanted to give up my career, but at that point I would have thrown it all away for him if I had to. Perhaps he needed to know that he was my number one priority in order for him to change, too.

A few days later, Grant moved back in, and we began again. It felt like a fresh start, and I was optimistic and hopeful. When I think about the incredibly life-altering decision that we made to stick it out, stay together, and choose each other every day, I can't help but also think about how different the trajectory of my life would have been if we'd made a different choice. During that time, I thought about my options and remembered a passage from one of my favorite authors, Lewis Carroll.

Alice came to a fork in the road. "Which road do I take?"
she asked. "Where do you want to go?" responded the Cheshire
cat. "I don't know," Alice answered. "Then," said the cat, "it
doesn't matter."

To me, it mattered. Being with Grant mattered. Staying
married to him mattered. I knew where I wanted to go.

Grant and I slowly became inseparable again. It wasn't
the type of raw and passionate love where I felt like I
couldn't live without him. It was the type of grounded
love that I knew I could live without but was choosing
not to. We did simple things, like making each other coffee in the morning and finding time to connect each day,
and big things, like planning a trip *together* for the upcoming New York Fashion Week. The biggest change was that
Grant and I were recommitted to our marriage and to each
other, and this shifted everything.

I was equally committed to the boundaries I had set up
around my work and private life, and this changed the energy around Grant and me, too. The world wouldn't crum-
ble if I held something back and kept it sacred instead of
sharing every detail with my readers. If anything, holding
up these boundaries would allow me to be more authentic.

Living my own truth meant being honest with myself
from that day forward. Fixing my marriage didn't save me.
But fixing myself did save my marriage. If I hadn't worked
on my personal healing, I doubt Grant and I would have
made it.

I continued working with my therapist every week, not
wanting to rush back into my relationship with Grant and
make the same mistakes twice. Grant and I also practiced

a new way of communicating that Dr. Meyer taught us. Once a day, we sat down face-to-face, with our legs and arms uncrossed, and gave each other five minutes of un-interrupted time to talk while the other just listened. The work we did together, combined with my own personal work, made all the difference. I journaled every morning and made sure to carve out at least one hour of alone time away from both Grant and my social media accounts to get in tune with myself every day.

Slowly, the feelings of wanting to run and hide or feel nothing at all lifted. I knew now that there was no one person or trip or outfit or award that would ever make me happy. It truly did have to start from within me. Once I gave myself the space and freedom to accept this message, the rest fell into place effortlessly.

That fall, Grant willingly suggested that he join me at New York Fashion Week. It was a huge deal to me that Grant was coming along, and I hoped it would be fun for him, too. I didn't care what he wore, but I wanted Grant to feel as good about his outfits as I did about mine. He had always hated shopping, but he loved it when I bought him new clothes. So, before we left, I ordered a bunch of things online that I thought he might like. Then I turned my office into a styling suite. I pulled out two rolling racks and hung up several pairs of pants, shirts, and blazers, simi-lar to a store layout. I also unboxed a few pairs of shoes and placed them on top of the boxes. I organized sunglasses, ties, and a few other accessories on a desk. Then I called him in.

"Mr. Grant! I'm ready for you," I said, and he came into the office. His smile was huge as he took in everything I'd bought for him. One by one, he tried everything on and started getting really into it. "I guess that one's a keeper," I said as he did a little jiggly dance wearing a black blazer by rag & bone.

A few days later, I left for New York with Haleigh to tackle the bulk of the fashion week work and chaos. The plan was for Grant to bring Polly and join me five days later. I was excited to introduce him to New York Fashion Week and planned a bunch of fun things for us to do together whenever I wasn't working, which wouldn't be often. In addition to all the regular shows and posted content, I was invited to the Tom Ford show for the first time and the show for Creatures of Comfort, a brand I had been wearing for years. I went backstage at the Tory Burch show and interviewed her for the blog, attended a luncheon for Bobbi Brown, and a presentation for Kate Spade.

Haleigh and I were driving around the city from sunup to sundown as I changed outfits and posted branded content on the way from one event to the next. Instagram Stories didn't exist yet, so I had also decided to create a fashion week vlog to give my followers a behind-the-scenes look at fashion week. When I got back to the hotel at the end of the day, I spent hours editing everything I'd filmed.

The week was hectic and exhausting, but I felt grounded in a new way. Grant and I were in regular contact, and knowing that he was on his way to join me helped me be fully present. I wasn't reading hateful comments or worrying about where I was seated at shows. I was too busy tapping into my creativity and pouring my whole self into my work. It felt fantastic.

I was in the back of the car with Haleigh, changing from an extremely snug matching plaid top and bottom by Tory Burch into a sporty Athleta outfit that we needed to shoot in Central Park for a sponsored post, when Grant called me after boarding the plane to New York. "We're about to take off," he told me as I pulled my sports bra over my head. "Check your Instagram."

I looked at Haleigh quizzically once the bra was in place. That was a weird request. Grant wasn't even on Instagram or any social media. I know it's silly, but it had always bothered me that other bloggers' husbands posted about their wives and Grant was basically a ghost.

I opened Instagram and saw that Grant had created an Instagram profile and tagged me in a post of him and Polly on their way to New York to be with me. I put my hand to my mouth and blinked back tears, not wanting to mess up the makeup I'd had done at five o'clock that morning. Yes, it was just an Instagram post, but I knew it was Grant's way of saying, *I'm here. I'm a part of your world.* And that meant everything.

Over the next few days, Grant was able to see my work in action for the first time. He had heard me talk about fashion week hundreds of times, but there was nothing like experiencing it firsthand. He couldn't believe how much work went into all of it, and he was equally surprised by how much he enjoyed being there.

When we got out of the car at the Ralph Lauren show, there were dozens of street-style photographers calling my name and snapping my picture. Grant was in shock. "I'm so proud of you, babe," he told me as the car pulled away from the curb. "I had no idea it was like this." I simply let out a smile as I leaned in to kiss him.

At the end of every New York Fashion Week is the big *Harper's Bazaar* ICONS party, a black-tie blowout event. I had been attending the event for a few years, but of course, this was Grant's first time going with me, and it felt like Grant's coming-out party. After taking photos on the red carpet, we made our way up the grand staircase. Several mega-influencers (with millions and millions of followers) were awed by Grant's appearance. They stopped, asked to take photos with us, and told him how happy they were to finally meet Jacey's elusive husband.

We made our way to the grand ballroom that was dimly lit with gorgeous huge chandeliers on the ceiling. A large circular bar in the middle of the room had tiers like a wedding cake, dressed in bottles of Moët & Chandon champagne. Kendall Jenner, Bella Hadid, Heidi Klum, and Nicki Minaj were only a few of the celebrities we spotted while we mixed and mingled. Just as Christina Aguilera hit the stage to perform, Grant and I sneaked out the back door to head to a dinner reservation we'd been looking forward to. It felt sneaky and fun to have something that we felt was even more important than the most highly sought-after New York Fashion Week event.

Hand in hand, all dressed up in our black tie, we walked from the Plaza Hotel to my favorite restaurant in New York, The Polo Bar. It was dark and cozy and romantic as we sat at the bar, enjoying a drink before dinner. We ordered pigs in a blanket as an appetizer, which we felt silly eating all dressed up in black tie.

When I lifted my napkin, I saw a little jewelry box hidden under there. "What's this?" I had no clue how Grant had sneaked it under the napkin without me noticing.

"Open it," he said. Inside the box was a simple gold band with quilted detailing from Chanel. It was the Coco Crush ring, one I'd secretly been coveting for years. I had no idea how Grant knew how much I loved those rings. I'm not an easy person to surprise, but I was truly shocked and touched. Grant lifted his glass for a toast as I slipped the ring onto my finger, stacking it over my wedding band to cement it in place.

"I want this ring to serve as a new promise," he said, looking in my eyes, "that we will continue to choose each other every day forever. No matter what," he continued, "I choose you, again and again."

I didn't bother fighting back my tears as I told Grant how much it all meant to me: his words, the ring, but mostly him just being there with me in every way. To me, the ring represented a fresh start in our commitment to one another. It was a symbol of what it really meant to be married, which I hadn't fully realized when I first took my vows. With that ring, we made our own renewal, fully owning and meaning those vows for the first time.

My favorite picture of Grant and me from that night is a random candid shot my photographer snapped as we were walking into the ICONS party when Grant said something funny. In the picture, I'm in a long gold dress by Michelle Mason and Grant is in his tux. We're holding hands and looking straight at each other, stopped right in the middle of the crosswalk of a bustling New York City street. When I look at that picture, I think of what Elizabeth Gilbert says in *Eat, Pray, Love* about how much she loves the Italian word *attraversiamo*, which means *let's cross over*. It was indeed a moment when Grant and I crossed over into a new level of commitment, beginning a fresh new chapter in our journey together.

10

The Northern Lights

I PUT MY HAND OVER MY MOUTH AS I STOOD IN THE doorway of the huge walk-in closet in our suite at The Peninsula Hotel in Paris. The French online retailer 24 Sèvres, which carried high-end labels like Louis Vuitton, Dior, Celine, and Moynat, had filled the entire closet with some of the most remarkable clothes, bags, and shoes I had ever seen—all in my size.

"Oh. My. Gawd," I said to Grant, running my hands over the luxe fabrics. I pulled a blue dress with floral detail off the hanger and held it up against me as I looked in the full-length mirror. "This is from the newest Erdem collection!"

I couldn't believe that this was all here for me. It was such ridiculous, over-the-top pampering that I had to laugh, imagining what Farm Girl Jacey would have thought if she could see this closetful of gorgeous clothes, all laid out for her. After I had pored through and gawked over every item in the closet, Grant and I stood on the balcony, looking out at the incredible view of the Eiffel Tower, and toasted to Paris with glasses of champagne. We were there for couture fashion week, which was a separate fashion week just for haute couture brands like Chanel and Dior. I had not been to couture week before, only ready-to-wear. It was work, of course, but it also felt like a mini-honeymoon. Everything felt like a honeymoon now that Grant and I were really, truly together.

My mind flashed back to the last time I had stared out at that same view, when I was in Paris with Haleigh. Only a year had passed since then, but so much had changed—not just my relationship with Grant and with my work, but, even more important, my relationship with myself. I was able to fully appreciate and enjoy the moment because I was back in my own skin. The numbness that had enveloped me for so long was gone, and I was finally feeling again.

No, that didn't mean that everything was suddenly perfect. Grant and I had a long road ahead of us, and I had a lot of work to do on myself as well. The healing had just begun, but it would continue. And the work we had done so far had made a marked difference.

For the first time, I had been invited to attend the Chanel show. Insert girlie scream here! All those trips to New York, all those meetings, and all the work I'd done to build up the brand had finally paid off.

And I almost missed it.

"Jacey! What time is the show?" Grant jerked out of bed the next morning in a panic. I looked at the clock out of one eye and saw that I had overslept by an hour. Thankfully, I had tried on my outfit the night before, and by then I had mastered the art of getting ready fast. I took a deep breath in through my nose and out through my mouth. "Don't panic," I told myself, knowing that I'd be able to get ready much faster if I stayed calm.

After doing a very simple and quick hair and makeup routine, I pulled up a pair of black opaque tights I had scored from Zara and struggled to tuck a long-sleeved black cotton T-shirt from Old Navy into the tights. Then I carefully pulled the sheer black tulle skirt that Chanel had sent me over my legs and nervously zipped it up the back. Finally, it was time for the icing on the cake. I reached for the metallic silver Chanel blazer and matching handbag the Chanel team had sent over to me the day before. The sleeves of the jacket were a bit frayed from past borrowers, but I still handled the exquisite piece as if it were made of glass as I slipped my arms through the sleeves and let it rest on my shoulders.

As I walked through the doors of the Grand Palais for the show just a few minutes later, I was faced with the back of a set of bleachers, just like at the football stadium back home. At most shows, I was seated in the front row, but this was Chanel. I was happy to have my seat toward the back.

I walked up to the top of the stairs, and a new world was revealed to me. I squinted my eyes in awe. The set included cascading waterfalls that trickled against a tall canyon, which served as a backdrop to the runway. The models walked along a wooden dock that was built above a meandering stream with trees and lush greenery peeking out. It was a magical woodland. I breathed in the clean air and could feel the mist from the waterfall kiss my cheek. I looked up at the crystal clear blue sky that beamed through the glass roof. It was overwhelmingly beautiful.

One by one, the models appeared from behind the waterfall and made their way up to the second runway, which met the first row of the set of bleachers I was sitting in. With each passing model, three rows' worth of cell phones attached to the arms of the attendees in front of me went up and down in unison. I giggled at how ridiculous it looked, and I realized that I looked just as ridiculous to the people behind me. There we all were at the Chanel fashion week show in Paris, looking ridiculous.

Fumbling between my cell phone and Canon camera, I did my best to get videos, photos, Snapchats, Instagram Stories, and Boomerangs of the models as they walked by. It all happened so fast, and before I knew it, the models were making their final walk through. Karl Lagerfeld came out and waved, and the thousands of people in the crowd began to make their way out onto the street.

The show was incredible and inspiring, almost like seeing a Beyoncé concert. But I kept waiting to feel the high I was used to experiencing after major career milestones. It never came. As I walked back to the hotel to tell Grant about the show, I realized that I wasn't feeling the low that usually followed the high, either. With my entire life more stable and grounded, I had finally broken free of that cycle of extreme highs and lows. I could enjoy things and work hard and feel happy and experience sadness, but I wasn't addicted to the roller-coaster ride anymore. I smiled to myself as I passed my reflection in a storefront, all dressed up in Chanel. I was grateful to be there, and even more grateful that it wasn't all that mattered to me anymore.

The other highlight of fashion week was a lavish black-tie party thrown by Dior. This year it was a masquerade ball. My relationship with Dior had evolved quite a lot over the years. When I first named my blog *Damsel in Dior*, I was trying to evoke an aspirational feeling. I never dreamed that I would literally be attending Dior events, much less dressed by the brand itself.

The first few times someone from the Dior team reached out to me, I was worried that they were going to ask me to change the name of my blog. In fact, I procrastinated before getting back to them in fear that they were going to serve me with papers or a lawsuit. I would have been willing to change the name. I just didn't want to face the embarrassment. When I finally met with the Dior team, I was pleasantly relieved to learn that they not only liked the name of my blog, but they said that I did a wonderful job representing the Dior brand. It was the greatest compliment of my career.

Even then, I wasn't sure whether or not Dior was going to dress me for the party. It wasn't something I would ever take for granted. My contact at Dior had told me that they were sending something over, but less than an hour before the party, nothing had arrived. I wasn't sure what to do.

It felt presumptuous to call Dior and ask where my dress was. But I had to get ready.

I called the front desk and begged them to let me know right away if something showed up for me. I checked my phone a hundred times and paced around our gorgeous suite while Grant sat in his tux, calmly waiting. Finally, I gave up and put on a lovely one-shouldered dress from Lanvin.

Just as I finished getting ready, my contact at Dior called. "I'm so sorry," she said in her lovely French accent. "Your dress is on its way." I looked at the time. We had to leave in thirty minutes, and I had no idea what this dress looked like or if it would even fit. But it was Dior. What could I say except "thank you"?

A few minutes later, the most beautiful black ball gown I had ever seen arrived. It had ruffled shoulders and a deep V in the front, and the skirt had layers and layers of tulle. By some miracle, it fit me perfectly, like it was made for me. It was one of my favorite dresses I'd ever worn. I felt like Cinderella as I slipped on the dress, strapped a beaded mask around my eyes, and we headed out to the ball.

It was an incredibly lavish evening, with music and oysters and champagne and celebrities as far as I could see. Grant and I laughed and danced and drank and schmoozed. I wasn't thinking about who might be talking behind my back or posting on *The Forum* about the one or two cigarettes I sneaked late in the evening. I was too busy being happy and actually living my life to worry about any of that. I had been wearing a mask in public for years, and ironically, that night with a literal mask on, I felt free to stop hiding.

The next morning, we woke up to the news that 24 Sèvres, the retailer that had hooked me up with all of those clothes, was sending Grant and me on a whirlwind two-day trip to Marrakesh. They had seen a few of my Instagram posts wearing the clothes they'd sent and wanted to keep the momentum going. It was spring in Paris, 24 Sèvres wanted to push their summer line, and it was hot in Marrakesh. I could post pictures of myself wearing the summer line in beautiful Moroccan locations. It took about thirty seconds to convince Grant, and off to Marrakesh we went!

I had always dreamed of going to Morocco and was in absolute heaven as we explored stunningly tiled palaces, wove our way through the old market, relaxed at the hotel's pool and spa, and enjoyed dinner and drinks with breathtaking sunset views. Everything in Marrakesh was so grand. Grant and I shared long romantic dinners, talking about what our future would look like. We laughed our way across the snake charmers in the Marrakesh square, Jemaa el-Fna. Grant was terrified of snakes, and seeing his reaction made me hoot with laughter.

The trip was so generous, but it wasn't a coincidence that 24 Sèvres was sending Grant and me away together now. The picture I had posted of the two of us crossing the street in New York had gotten a bigger reaction from my followers than anything I'd ever posted before. To date, it was my most liked post on Instagram.

Little by little, I started sharing more of our lives together with my followers. With Grant around more and nothing to hide, he naturally started showing up on the blog and in my pics and videos. At first, he was like a supporting character in the background, and I always asked for his approval before posting anything that included him. There were some moments that he asked we reserve for just us instead of sharing them with my followers, and I respected his wishes. I was just so happy to have him involved at all, and never wanted to push him too hard.

Despite his hesitance to be in the spotlight, Grant was always himself on camera—charming and witty and a little bit shy—and my followers fell in love with him. Whenever Grant showed up in a video, they commented, asking to see more of him. He almost never posted on Instagram himself, but I didn't care. I didn't want him to do anything he didn't want to do.

Before long, the brands I was working with also started noticing how great Grant was. Some sent him gifts like clothes and ski gear, assuming that we'd feature them on the blog. Others asked for Grant to appear in sponsored posts along with me. After a while, some brands started reaching out to Grant directly, offering to dress him for fashion week or to see if he was interested in shooting content for them.

In my career, I have learned that the things that happen the most naturally, with the least amount of stress and pressure, are the ones that are meant to be. It's no coincidence that the most successful brand deals I've done are also the easiest to work on. The opposite is also true. There have been so many partnerships that I've fought for and that didn't end up taking off because they hadn't come together naturally.

It took me a long time to learn this lesson, to start listening to my instincts and stop trying to force things. When I was starting out, I wanted Grant to be a part of the blog so badly, but he didn't have time, he didn't want to do it, and it didn't feel natural to him. I could see now that it simply wasn't the right time. It probably wouldn't have worked if I had managed to strong-arm it into happening.

When we started to repair our relationship, Grant had just completed some big real-estate development projects in Culver City. He was still doing property management, but because of the real-estate market in LA, he decided not to take on any new projects right away. So he was around more, observing and learning about the day-to-day reality of my business. I started to include him in daily conversations and decision-making, and then I started cc'ing him on things to keep him in the loop.

It was a natural progression. As the brands got to know Grant, they loved the fact that he was a down-to-earth, regular guy with his own hobbies because it opened them up to new types of exposure. Grant started to brainstorm projects that aligned with his personal interests, and he found that he was good at it. Soon, he was developing his own relationships and deals.

Ironically, I started to feel protective over him. It was one thing when brands gifted him clothes, but when they started offering to pay for him to appear in my content, I was hesitant. I had spent eight years feeling hyperconscious of how I looked in pictures and how I was being perceived. I didn't want to do that to Grant. But he was surprisingly game, especially when he saw that we could charge double my regular fee for a sponsored post with the two of us in it.

While Grant was slowly but steadily becoming a part of Damsel Inc., there was another change happening within the industry. The days of fashion bloggers posing in front of the Eiffel Tower in Sarah Jessica Parker–style tutus seemed to be ending, and more organic, in-the-moment content was becoming en vogue. This was perfect for me because now Grant was around to take photos in real time. Instead of having to hire a photographer and change outfits a hundred times during a full-on photo shoot, I could just go about my day while Grant snapped pics in real time. Grant wasn't a photographer, and it was a process of trial and error for him to learn how to take photos that worked for the blog and social media, but it paid off with content that looked so much more natural and allowed us to enjoy our time together in the moment.

We were having dinner at home one night when Grant told me that he had decided not to take on any more projects with his company. This wasn't news to me. He had said something similar shortly after fashion week. For years, while I was globe-hopping, Grant had been stressed and unhappy with his career. He never lit up when he talked about his projects, and he was frustrated that he didn't have much of a chance to express his creative side.

"It's more fun and we're more productive when we're working on *Damsel* together," he told me now.

"That's for sure," I said.

"So, let's make it official."

I looked up and saw a smile on Grant's face. "You mean it?" I asked. I had wanted Grant to become a full-time part of the brand for so long, but now I wanted to make sure it was what he really wanted, too. His smiling, nodding face told me all I needed to know.

"That's great news!" I dug into my food, feeling such relief and excitement for both of us. Grant is one of the most creative, passionate, and talented people I know. He has always had the best ideas for creative projects, and I knew that working together would benefit the brand and be more fulfilling for Grant personally.

Although we agreed to make it official, we didn't give Grant a title or a business card, because we felt silly doing that. He just became a part of the team. Not only was Grant great at helping me negotiate better deals and set boundaries with work, but he was also far more skilled as a COO than I was. He was a pro at dealing with employees, accounting, and time management, and started taking a more active role in running all the behind-the-scenes.

It felt like a natural and easy progression. While we used to argue about Grant not being involved and not knowing about every project I was working on, we were now able to connect and bond over discussions about work, projects, and creative ideas.

I was right. (Of course!) With Grant involved, business was booming. I also found that being at home more allowed me to dedicate more of my time to the creative part of the business—ideas for partnerships and sponsored content and gift guides. By being still, I was ironically doing more, while I had always thought that the best way to work hard was by wearing myself out, traveling around the world. It was a lovely surprise to see that without the extreme highs and lows in my life, I was better able to focus. As a result, I was more productive. I was also bringing my whole self and true confidence to my work, which made everything work better. Maya Angelou said, "Nothing will work unless you do," and I was seeing this clearly for myself.

Having Grant involved also helped me to see things from a different perspective. Suddenly, we had more brand deals than ever, more engagement on social media, and more views on the website. It was so much to keep track of, even for both of us.

I'd been burned by the management company and was determined to keep managing everything ourselves. That is, until things started falling through the cracks. After forgetting to post sponsored content and almost losing out on a deal with Volvo because I couldn't keep up with my emails, I finally admitted that we needed help.

Not long before, I had spoken on a panel at a blogging conference with Katherine Schwarzenegger and had met her manager, Hilary, who seemed like a boss. She had asked me to grab lunch, and I'd never followed up with her because I was so busy. But I tracked her email down and agreed to meet with her.

I was still hesitant about hiring someone to represent me, and it didn't help when I learned that Hilary worked for the same management company I'd met with before. I didn't want to be just another notch on their belt. But

Hilary won me over. She told me that she had only a small handful of clients on her roster, and she wanted me to be one of them. Most of all, I liked her and wanted to work with her, so I agreed to give it a shot.

Yes, I was working on myself, but I was still a micro-manager and a perfectionist. It was incredibly hard for me to let go of the reins and hand them over to Hilary. At first, I insisted that Grant and I were cc'd on every email she sent, and I was on the phone with Hilary constantly. We talked almost every day to go over every offer, every email, and every thought about a potential brand partnership or idea about how to develop my brand further. I was so used to being in control of every single aspect of the company. Plus, I had worked so hard to establish and maintain my relationships in the industry. It was difficult to trust them to anyone.

Hilary proved herself very quickly. During New York Fashion Week that September, we had twenty deals going down, and with Hilary negotiating, I was earning more than ever before for each of them. I realized that having Hilary on board allowed her to go to bat for me and freed me up to focus on the creative and fun parts of the collaborations.

Amazingly, with both Grant's and Hilary's involvement, after fashion week my longtime bucket-list goal of earning a million dollars of revenue in a year was within reach. As we worked around the clock on the holiday campaigns and Twelve Days of Damsel giveaways, Hilary was negotiating a new deal with Amazon to promote the Echo Dot.

One night, we were working late, as usual, when Hilary called me. "Put me on speaker," she said.

I did as she said, and then Hilary told me to check my email. I sat down at my desk, opened my email, and scrolled through until I saw one from Hilary with the subject Amazon Deal. When I saw the number listed on the email, I banged my fist on my desk in excitement.

"Get Grant in here," I told Haleigh, and when he joined us in the office, I screamed, "We did it! The Amazon deal pushed us over the edge!"

We all cheered and tried our best at an awkward three-way hug before Grant went into the kitchen to get champagne. He came back with three glasses and toasted, "To *Damsel*."

"To *Damsel*," I repeated, looking at Grant. "We made this happen together."

Hitting that milestone was definitely a peak, and it was very exciting, but I knew by then that work alone wouldn't sustain that feeling. To be truly fulfilled, I needed something more in my life. My relationship with Grant felt solid and steady, but within a few months, I started to feel like something was still missing.

Ever since my miscarriage, Grant and I had revisited the idea of having a baby each year. Every time we sat down to have the conversation, we agreed that the time wasn't right and that we would give it another year and see how we felt then. Of course, for a long time I had been telling myself that things weren't right between me and Grant, and that's why we weren't having kids. But now I knew we were in a good place. And I was starting to feel like a child was the thing that was missing from our family. So, why did I still not feel ready?

There were practical reasons for my doubts. I had been watching carefully to see what happened to other bloggers after they had kids, and the truth is that most of them ended up dropping off. I didn't see a road map for how to stay successful in this business while being a mom. This confirmed what my own mom had always told me when I was growing up—to achieve everything I wanted to before having a child. She felt that she had given up her dreams to have a family and drilled it into me not to do the same thing.

I also had fears that ran deeper. I was finally getting to know myself and could not deny my tendency to hyper-focus and lose myself in whatever I took on. This aspect of my ADHD was a blessing when it came to my business, but how would it affect me as a mom? I was terrified that if I had a child, I would put everything into motherhood and lose my connection to myself. It was hard enough for me to find some semblance of work/life balance. How would a child factor into that equation? Would I end up smothering my child and losing my entire identity to being a mom? Would becoming a mother take away from my beautiful, albeit selfish, life?

Amid these thoughts, Grant and I were invited to the Four Seasons Resort Lanai, on a tiny Hawaiian island next to Maui. Even after we agreed to go on the trip, these questions still circulated in my mind. Would we be able to go on trips like this if we had a child? Now that Grant and I were traveling together, these trips were magical. We would have a few days to explore, swim, hike, and relax together while shooting content for the blog.

We were halfway to Hawaii and had fully settled into our seats on the plane, cruising at altitude, when, out of nowhere, the plane just dropped. Boom. I can't even explain how sudden and terrifying it was. Of all the flights I had taken over the years, I had never ever experienced anything like that. It felt like we had fallen hundreds of feet. Then it happened again. And again.

My hands gripped on to Grant's arm. My knuckles were white. All around me was panic. Everyone was screaming. The flight attendants dropped their facade and showed sheer terror on their faces. I clutched on to Grant for dear life, feeling positive in my gut that we were going down.

Spoiler alert: We didn't go down. And I know this will sound cheesy. But those minutes of turbulence when I truly thought I was about to die forced me to see my life in the bigger picture, and I knew I would regret it if I didn't have a child.

At my first appointment with my therapist after the trip, I told her about how conflicted I was feeling, and she recommended that we do a guided meditation. I settled into my chair as she asked me to go in my mind to a place that brought me peace. My mind immediately flashed to Concan, Texas, a river town in Hill Country where my family vacationed every summer when I was a child. My grandparents owned a cabin on the river, and my brother and I often stayed with them. We spent all day collecting heart-shaped rocks, and when I got homesick, my grandfather told me adventure stories about a family of frogs who lived on the river. It was so peaceful there in nature, and I felt that tranquil feeling in my body now as I imagined myself there.

"Someone is coming to give you a message," my therapist said.

At first, I didn't see anyone. I just let my mind drift. And then, suddenly, my Meme appeared, holding out a heart-shaped rock. I took it from her and we sat by the river and talked. I told her that I was scared of having kids and, true to real-life Meme, she gave me a stern Southern talking-to.

"This is your life," she told me, kindly but firmly. "Stop messing around, and do what you want to do. I want to meet my great-grandchild before I die."

Just as quickly as she'd appeared, Meme was gone, and I was back in my therapist's office. "She's right," I said. "What am I waiting for?"

Grant and I agreed to start trying. We had no idea if I could get pregnant naturally or how long it would take. First, I had a trip scheduled to Paris for fall fashion week. Grant didn't come with me this time because he had a big trip planned with his friends, and Haleigh didn't, either. For the first time in a while, I was traveling alone. And while I was fine with them not coming, I felt homesick and slightly melancholy on the long-haul flight.

I tried to sleep on the plane, but was tossing and turning. There was a gentleman in front of me talking loudly. His voice was deep and muffled, and I could not make out a word of what he was saying. But he was speaking excitedly about something. Then the woman he was talking to lifted her window shade.

My brain was still fuzzy, but suddenly I just knew. My heart skipped a beat as I rushed to lift the shade next to my seat. I could not believe what my eyes met. There they were—the northern lights. The Big Dipper was crowned perfectly on top of the aurora. Or was it the Little Dipper? It didn't matter either way. It was the most beautiful thing I had ever seen. I pressed my nose up to the cool glass. A soft glow danced through the stars, creating waves of magic. It was just as my dad had always described it.

Using my hands to create a shield around my eyes, I could see more clearly how the muted gray tones melted together into a sea of light. A symphony of stars and glowing light spread across the sky. Even though I was alone in my seat, it felt like everyone I loved most was right there with me, enjoying it, too, and that everything in my life was on the right path again, following the stars in the sky.

"Wish I may, wish I might," I murmured to myself, gazing out the airplane window. I could not believe my eyes. "Have the wish I wish tonight."

I felt a light bounce of turbulence beneath my seat, and I was taken right back to our bouncy trampoline, where time stood still, where my dad's stories were the most brilliant in the world, and my mom's laughter was like a warm hug on a chilly winter night. It was in that exact moment that I realized the wish being granted was no longer the prize.

A month later, I was pregnant.

11

Pulling Back the Curtain

MY BELOVED POLLY WAS THE RUNT OF HER LITTER, and she spent her whole life riddled with health issues. She was allergic to the type of protein found in almost all dog food and could only eat fish, and she still required steroid treatments for her allergies. Then there were side effects from the steroids. Her health had finally stabilized right around the time that I found out I was pregnant. Then, suddenly, she started getting horrible tumors on her paws. They looked like giant blisters, and she licked them until they bled. Then as soon as one wound healed, a new one immediately popped up in its place.

Besides my concerns about Polly, it was such a happy time. I was keeping up the pace at work and maintaining my emotional boundaries, Grant and I were in a good place, and we were both thrilled about the pregnancy. Of course, it also came with its share of challenges. I had pretty bad morning sickness and was suddenly so emotional that I cried over every little thing. It was still early on in the pregnancy, so Grant and I were keeping the news to ourselves, and it felt good to have our own delicious, happy secret.

The pregnancy also made me feel even more protective over Polly. You won't be surprised to hear that as soon as I saw her first blister, I dived down an endless rabbit hole, looking for a diagnosis and cure for her tumors. After dozens of trips back and forth to the vet, we took her to a specialist in San Diego to perform a surgery that removed the inside webbing of her paws. Then they sent the tumors to a lab to be tested.

Throughout this whole process, I was posting about Polly's health on social media in real time. I posted about the tumors. I posted about the surgery. And a few weeks later, when the vet got the results of the lab testing, I posted from the parking lot, saying that we were finally about to find out what was going on with Polly. Then I went in, and the vet told me that Polly's tumors were cancerous and she only had about two months to live.

In a state of shock, I went home and curled up with Polly in my bed. She could barely walk and had all four of her paws wrapped up in bandages. Yet I felt blindsided. Of course, I had known there was a chance it was cancer, but besides the tumors, Polly seemed completely like her normal self. I had convinced myself that it wasn't anything serious.

Grant came into the room and found me in a heap, sobbing. "Jace, it's going to be okay," he told me. "We'll get a second opinion. The cancer hasn't spread, so maybe it's not as bad as they're saying." I just nodded and continued crying. It wasn't like me to break down so easily, but pregnancy hormones are real. "In the meantime," Grant continued, sounding a bit trepidatious, "have you checked the blog?"

I looked at him. No, I hadn't checked the blog, but I grabbed my laptop. From Grant's tone, I assumed I was going to find something bad, but instead I saw dozens of comments on my last post about Polly, asking for an update on the test results. My readers had been going along on this journey with me, and they were waiting with bated breath for Polly's results.

I didn't know what to say or do. I didn't want to post about the cancer before emotionally processing the news myself, or before getting a second opinion. I told myself that the cancer might turn out to be treatable, and then I might be putting my readers through an emotional roller coaster for no reason. But I also knew I couldn't leave them hanging for much longer.

I took a moment to get myself together, and then I threw on my sunglasses and went outside. Grant took a picture of me with Polly that made it look like we were just getting home from the vet, and I posted it with an apology for taking so long to send an update. I said that we still didn't have clear answers, but we were getting closer and

I would keep everyone posted. Like I said, don't believe everything you see on social media!

I wasn't trying to lie to my followers. Quite the opposite, actually. I learned from this experience with Polly not to post things in real time that could potentially have a negative outcome. As I started sharing things after I'd processed them with a little bit of hindsight, I was able to be more honest than ever.

The timing of this lesson could not have been better, as I was considering how to handle announcing my pregnancy. I was still very worried about how being pregnant and being a mom would affect my career, how the brands I worked with and my followers alike would react to the news. Would they see a pregnancy announcement and think, *Welp, there goes her career,* or see me as *just* a mom now? Would brands still want to work with me when I no longer fit in their sample sizes or represented their carefree, young target demographic?

I decided to hire a very popular business consultant named Idalia, who was working with top-tier bloggers throughout the world. My hope was for her to help me work through the process, and she affirmed my fears that brands would *not*, in fact, want to keep working with me, at least while I was pregnant. *Gee, thanks.* Yes, I had thought this was the case, but it was still shocking to hear. Nevertheless, it forced me to come up with a plan.

For one thing, Idalia advised me to wait for as long as possible to announce the pregnancy. At first, it felt strange to be keeping such a big part of my happiness from my followers, but I knew in my heart that she was right. Even though I was nauseous all the time, I was truly happy, with a new light in my eyes and excitement in my heart that I longed to share. But I also saw it as a way of protecting my family, by keeping this miraculous new being that Grant and I had created as something truly sacred and shared only by the two of us.

For the first few months of my pregnancy, I kept my head down and focused on work and Polly's health. Knowing that I would have to hide the pregnancy once I started showing, I took tons of pictures of myself before my body started changing. This was honestly the *last thing* I wanted to do during the end of my first trimester. I was exhausted, and I didn't want my content to feel inauthentic. But at the end of the day, posting a previously shot "going out" photo on a Friday night when I was really feeling sick in bed was better than posting nothing at all.

I also shot the content for all the deals we had already booked, even though they wouldn't go live for months. Throughout the pregnancy, Grant and I filmed every pregnancy milestone, doctor's visit, test result, and ultrasound, but we kept it all to ourselves to be shared with the world later.

Meanwhile, I threw myself into researching Polly's condition and finding alternative treatments for her cancer. I got multiple opinions, found a holistic vet to treat her without surgery, and created a bucket list for the rest of Polly's life, which included going with us on a trip to Italy, eating lots of ice cream, and taking daily walks around the block, even if that meant pulling her in a wagon. She lived for three more years, and in retrospect, I am so glad that

I never shared the news that she only had two months to live. This showed me yet again that life is better presented with the benefit of hindsight to enlighten each moment.

As my pregnancy progressed, my physical and emotional symptoms increased significantly. And to make things worse, I constantly judged myself for not being able to handle it better. I had this image in my mind of what my pregnancy should be like: me, glowing, with a perfectly round little baby bump and some quirky food cravings that Grant would find utterly adorable. He'd run out to get me Popeyes and ice cream in the middle of the night, and we'd eat it out of the carton in bed together, giggling with joy.

It...wasn't like that. I quickly found myself in an in-between phase of pregnancy. It looked like I had just eaten a few extra cheeseburgers but felt like I was carrying around a watermelon. I had a hard time accepting my changing body, and the internal dialogue that I was feeding myself was a cluster of self-hate mixed with self-pity and annoyance.

How did other women make this look so easy? I would open my IG feed to find my fellow bloggers, pregnant and taking morning jogs with their significant others. I could barely walk downstairs to the kitchen. All I wanted to do was eat, but it left me with a knot in my throat because I knew that it would only lead to more weight gain.

Even getting dressed, which used to be fun and creative, was suddenly fraught. On so many mornings, I found myself in tears over what to wear. Getting dressed every day was my job. It was how Grant and I paid our bills. If I didn't get up, get dressed, and smile for a photo, then we wouldn't make any money that day. The pressure was so intense, and I kept telling myself to get over it, that I should have just been grateful to be pregnant. And I was! But I felt miserable at the same time.

I imagine that my pregnancy would have been difficult under any circumstances, but layered on top of a job where I was constantly being evaluated based on my appearance and my clothes, it was incredibly challenging. Let's be real for a minute here. When brands dress an influencer, they send sample sizes, which are the same ones that go down the runway. That means they're a size zero or maybe a size two. So, what happens when that isn't your size because you're not actually a supermodel? Too bad for you. You have less access to high-end brands and fewer opportunities in the industry as a result.

It's no coincidence that everyone sitting in the front row of fashion shows is a size zero. They are there because they fit into the sample sizes and can showcase the brand's line just like the models on the runway. Thank goodness, things are slowly starting to shift now, but when I was coming up in this industry, I never saw plus-sized bloggers or even average-sized bloggers at fashion shows. We were all brainwashed into thinking that a size zero was the only acceptable size.

As my pregnancy progressed, I learned tricks to cover up my weight gain, like throwing a jacket over a dress that was unzipped in the back. Don't get me wrong. It was a luxury and a privilege to be dressed by these brands, but it was still demoralizing to be photographed wearing clothes that don't fit when my entire job is to look good and sell those items to the public. For the first time, I felt what it was like to literally not fit into this industry.

Many times during my pregnancy, I found myself sitting on my closet floor, realizing what so many women must feel every day. Of course, I should have known this sooner. I became angry that brands were forcing women to stoop to extreme measures to fit into an unrealistic ideal, or to hate themselves when they could not.

When women can't fit into clothing, why do we blame it on our own bodies instead of blaming it on the clothes? Women are constantly told to love our bodies at any size, putting the pressure on us instead of expecting brands to be more inclusive with their sizing and messaging so that we can achieve that self-love and acceptance. And all the unrealistic images that social media influencers and bloggers posted, yours truly included, only added fuel to the fire.

Around this time, I started to pay very close attention to which brands were size inclusive and make a point of trying to work with them. The goal of my blog had always been to make my readers feel good in their clothes and in their own skin. I didn't want to contribute to making women feel ashamed of their bodies or to make getting dressed a struggle for them.

At the same time, I was terrified that someone would notice that I looked different in a picture and guess that I was pregnant. I obsessed over every photo. Poor Grant had to reshoot me so many times and listen to me moan and yell when I thought I looked fat. I realize in retrospect that I should have been proud of my body. But so many years in this industry—and being a woman in this culture in general—had deeply ingrained the idea that one body type was the ideal and anything else was simply less than.

After I had used up all the content I'd pre-shot before I started showing, I learned every trick in the book to hide my pregnancy and weight gain in my pics. Most of the time, I could get away with simply sitting down with my arms draped in front of me, covering my stomach. Other times, I was strategic about repurposing old content. I didn't want the blog to feel dated or redundant, so I dug up photos from previous trips and photo shoots that I had never used and posted them now. Once in a while, I resorted to featuring a big bag that I placed in front of my belly. But none of these tricks solved the fact that the clothes the brands sent me to wear in my posts didn't fit! Eventually, I confided in some of them about my pregnancy, swearing them to secrecy.

Even though my rational mind knew that changes to my body were normal and inevitable and a sign that everything was progressing as it should, it felt awful. Nothing fit, nothing felt good, and my body didn't feel like my own anymore. Yet I still felt so much pressure to look perfect and "photo ready" all the time. On so many days, I turned my closet upside down and ended up sitting on the floor, crying with all my clothes in piles around me. It didn't help that my hormones were raging. I had absolutely no control over my body or my emotions.

One day, I pulled myself off my closet floor and went into the kitchen to get some ice water. But the ice was all clumped together, and something in me just snapped. All the pressure and stress came to a head. I took out the whole ice tray and slammed it onto the floor with every ounce of muscle in my body. I stared down at the floor in shock as the entire thing shattered.

Another day, I found a bunch of spiderwebs on the outdoor furniture on our porch, and I lost it, using all my might to throw the furniture off the porch and onto the lawn. The neighbors were outside, watching the whole thing, and once I calmed down, I was utterly mortified by my own behavior. Grant just watched with his eyes wide. These episodes were scary for him, and when he reacted with silence, I worried that he thought something was truly wrong with me.

Why am I telling you this? The entire time I was a hormonal, raging mess of a human, I was making it even harder by berating myself and wondering why I wasn't that perfect glowing pregnant princess that I'd expected to be. If some people do have easy fairy-tale pregnancies, I'm happy for them. But I don't want to hold up an unrealistic image of what pregnancy was like, or at least what it was like for me. Although I was still keeping the pregnancy between me and Grant, I knew that I would eventually write about it honestly so that my followers could gain a more accurate picture.

When I was five months pregnant and had already gained thirty pounds, I knew I couldn't hide the pregnancy much longer. As my emotional symptoms began to ease up a bit (thank God), I started gaining weight rapidly and experiencing more physical aches and pains. My belly had popped, and New York Fashion Week was right around the corner. It was the perfect time to announce the pregnancy and make a big splash. Despite how exhausted and achy I felt, I was determined to make a statement by rocking my pregnant belly during fashion week and proving to everyone (especially myself) that I still had it.

Before New York, I had work to do with Waldorf Astoria in Chicago. The (ridiculous) plan was for Grant, Polly, and me to all fly to Chicago together, spend two days shooting, fly back to LA for two days to get ready for fashion week, and then fly to New York. After Polly's cancer scare, I didn't want to travel without her. By our second day in Chicago, I was physically and emotionally exhausted. I just couldn't perform and be "on" all day like I used to. I know so many women have to do their jobs throughout their pregnancies—jobs that are much more physically demanding than mine. But my body just stopped and said no.

On our second day in Chicago, I could not get out of bed. My body was made of lead, and no matter how hard I tried, it would not move. I was having Braxton-Hicks contractions that were so intense, they scared not only me, but Grant, too. Grant called my doctor, who said that I was pushing myself too hard and that we should do whatever we could to make the trip a little easier on me. Grant suggested that I go straight to New York and rest while he went home and got everything ready for fashion week. The idea of Grant packing for me for New York Fashion Week was laughable and terrifying, but the idea of skipping the back-and-forth flights and having some time to recharge was too good to pass up.

Before we left Chicago and went our separate ways, we had one more important job to do. I needed the perfect picture for the pregnancy announcement I was planning to make right at the start of fashion week. Rather than panic and schedule a big photo shoot, I went to my camera roll and picked a photo that Grant and I had snapped the week earlier in front of a bathroom mirror in our house. We were posing very naturally with Grant's hand on my belly while he kissed me on the forehead. Instead of hiding my belly, I had highlighted it by wearing a clingy long-sleeved white dress and shooting my body in profile.

Once I landed in New York and Grant was in LA, we FaceTimed for three hours while I walked him through exactly what to pack. Let me just say, that man's patience is truly otherworldly. Then I slept for twelve hours and woke up feeling so much better.

Alone in the hotel room, I posted the picture announcing my pregnancy and then braced myself for the reaction. I knew the announcement would feel big, but as the likes and comments started blowing up on my feed, it felt bigger than big. Then my phone began erupting with texts and emails from fellow influencers, brands, and designers. Some sent flowers to me at the hotel and posted on their own accounts to congratulate me. The hotel's housekeepers even brought me flowers and extra pillows.

It was so affirming to receive so much warmth and excitement from my followers. They weren't upset that I had held out on them, and they didn't question what would happen to my career. They were just happy for me. I felt so loved and cared for, and immediately felt a huge wave of relief and hope for the industry, after all. My pregnancy was something to be proud of, not something I should have ever felt I needed to hide. My followers' affirmations helped give me the confidence I needed during this big transitional time in my life.

All day, I relaxed in the hotel room, ordered room service, and scrolled on my phone, soaking it in. Then the next day, I had back-to-back fittings and was smacked back down to reality. Nothing fit me. I had to keep asking for more options, and the brand reps were busy and overwhelmed and had no patience for this high-maintenance pregnant lady. It was awful to feel like my body was a nuisance, and I was worried that the brands would be turned off by this new version of me that couldn't gratefully accept the first outfit they offered. Why would they continue to dress me when there were hundreds of size-zero bloggers lined up behind me, ready and more than willing to take my spot?

Despite this constant anxiety, it was a relief after fashion week to not have to hide the pregnancy any longer. As predicted, much of my work did indeed drop off. The month after the announcement, I earned only 20 percent of the amount I had been earning each month for the previous year. This remained consistent throughout the rest of my pregnancy.

Even though I knew to expect this type of decrease, it was still shockingly disappointing. After so many years of posting, supporting, and promoting some of the biggest brand names in fashion, those same brands turned their backs on Pregnant Jacey. I had worked so hard to overcome my insecurities, but it was hard not to let this rock me. I practiced not identifying with the feelings that this was a sign of my inadequacy.

Deep down, I knew that it spoke volumes about the character of these brands instead of the fact that there was something wrong with me. But it left a bad taste in my mouth about working in an industry that was ultimately all about appearance. For the first time since starting the blog, I began to think about what it would mean to shift my career in some way. For the time being, I was grateful that Grant and I had planned ahead for this to happen by carefully budgeting and cutting back on our expenses, so I knew we could manage financially until I made a change or won my brand partners back after the baby was born.

Until then, I had one last trip planned to Paris to cover the Chanel show. I was six months pregnant and had made the horrible decision to cut my hair short. Never make a drastic change like that during pregnancy! I don't know if it was swelling from the flight or just more pregnancy weight gain, but I woke up on the morning of the show swollen and puffy and feeling awful. I hated my hair and nothing fit me, so I put on a comfortable printed dress from Zimmermann and threw a Chanel jacket on top of it. Not one street-style photographer took my photo on my way in or out of the show, and for the first time in my career, I failed to nail my coverage.

To cover a show like Chanel, I had to juggle my phone, my digital camera, and a video camera in my lap, trying to get at least two or three publishable shots, plus video. There was also a ton of pressure to get a "money shot" of a model or Karl Lagerfeld walking down the runway with perfect focus on a detail, accessory, or special moment from the show. The key was to post it quickly before someone else beat me to it and posted a similar picture.

That day, I fumbled my cameras, barely got one decent shot, and was late posting it because I was still hoping that I would manage to get something better. I hoped against hope that Chanel wouldn't notice my lackluster performance. I didn't get my answer until a year later when I wasn't invited back.

For the rest of my pregnancy, I stayed at home and tried to focus on work and taking care of myself. I was gaining weight rapidly, and although I was concerned and felt ill at ease in my own body, my doctor told me not to worry about it. So, after spending countless hours in front of the mirror studying the stretch marks forming on my legs and the new cellulite on my glutes, I finally left my closet, pulled out my laptop, and did the one thing that had always helped me get through tough moments: I wrote.

Lucky Charms and Frosted Flakes along with a gallon jug of milk are a few of the many things you would have never found in my pantry nine months ago. But carb-loading was the only thing that made me not nauseous during my first trimester of pregnancy. It was also one of the biggest things that made me feel emotionally unstable during that first trimester. A knot would form in my throat, fighting back the shame, as I poured a bowl of sugary breakfast to ward off morning sickness. The guilt I carried alongside my growing belly left me feeling insecure, ugly, and, well, fat.

When I moved to Los Angeles ten years ago, I didn't realize how much the city's "think thin" culture would imprint on my mind on a daily basis. For someone who loves staying physically fit and eating healthy, I truly appreciate the fact that in the middle of December I can go on a hike, find a delicious green juice, and have various fitness classes at my disposal. I also love that when my circle of girlfriends goes out to dinner, we talk about what we order and openly discuss how much we are working out.

Before I was pregnant, I considered myself to be conscious about my body image but not too self-conscious about my weight. I've never considered myself to be "fat" or hateful over the way I looked. But when my pregnancy test came back positive, I slowly but surely realized I was positively lying to myself. I noticed the voices constantly circulating in my head were hateful, shaming, and downright unhealthy.

There was one night in particular that changed everything for me. When I was around the four-month mark of my pregnancy, I went out to dinner with my family and ordered chicken-fried steak with gravy (I'm from the South). To add salt to my inner self-hate wounds, they all joked about my order, which was obviously more than what I'd typically eat. I know in my heart that my family didn't mean to hurt my feelings, but I went to bed feeling embarrassed and angry. I stayed awake, googling "how much weight should I gain while pregnant?" The average says twenty-five to thirty-five pounds. I cried myself to sleep, knowing I was already on track to be well above the average.

The next morning, I woke up puffy-eyed and with an extremely frustrated attitude about getting dressed. Nothing fit, nothing felt good, and my body didn't feel like my own anymore. I looked in the mirror and studied—truly *studied*—the forming stretch marks on my legs and cellulite on my glutes. I took a long, deep breath and something within me said *"let it go."* That was when I realized I had two choices: to wallow in self-pity and feel sorry for myself, or to shrug it off and accept my changing body.

I thought pregnancy was the one time in a woman's life when she didn't have to worry about weight gain, healthy eating habits, and working out. Boy, was I wrong! The truth is that no matter what, your life has to have balance—and mine didn't. I wasn't truly living a healthy lifestyle pre-pregnancy: I'd binge-eat pizza on a Sunday night with wine or diet Monday through Friday to get trim for bikini season. So when I got pregnant, I didn't know how to meet myself somewhere in the middle of making smart choices with food while also loving myself.

I waited to post about my weight gain until I had fully processed and embraced it. By then, I had gained sixty pounds in all and wanted to be up-front and take ownership of it. I was already pulling the wool over people's eyes by wearing a jacket over a dress that didn't fit. I didn't want to do the same thing with my entire pregnancy. Writing and sharing that essay was not only my way of finding self-acceptance, but also a way of hopefully reaching another pregnant woman out there who might be feeling the same insecurities as I was and helping her not feel so alone.

In addition to posting on my blog, I sent my article to the popular pregnancy website *The Bump*, which published it on their site. I was amazed to see how positively my readers responded and how many of them shared their own similar stories after reading mine. This empowered me to keep opening up about the struggles I faced during my last trimester—mostly pain and difficulty walking. I was diagnosed with Symphysis Pubis Dysfunction (SPD), which made my pelvic joints unstable and caused extreme pain that shot down the ligaments in my leg.

By the last month of my pregnancy, every moment brought its own unique agony. The less I moved, the less pain I felt. The less I moved, the further down a dark rabbit hole of depression I went. The only bright spot was that the more honest I was with my followers, the better of a response I got. They reached out, saying they had experienced similar pain, or simply to say thank you for painting an honest picture of what pregnancy looked like. For the first time, they saw me as a real human, flaws and all, and they accepted me anyway.

It felt strangely similar to the first time I had shared the truth about my dad's alcoholism at my sorority's candle-light circle. I was letting this community of women see me in a new way, too, and instead of turning away, they pulled me in closer. This helped give me the strength I needed to face the next chapter.

12

Damsel in Dior

IT IS EXACTLY TWENTY-THREE STEPS FROM THE SIDE of my bed to the toilet. I made this journey many times each night toward the end of my pregnancy. I was in so much pain that I honestly could not wait to give birth. I thought the delivery would mean the end of the physical discomfort I'd been in for nine long months. Once the baby was born, I was certain that I would be out of pain and able to focus on my new life as a mom.

I was due on January 31, and I was so huge and so uncomfortable toward the end that my doctor scheduled an induction for a week later in case I didn't go into labor on my own. Having that date on the calendar felt so freeing. I could count down the days, knowing I'd be out of pain by then. If you're a parent, right now you're laughing at me. Go ahead. But why didn't you tell me? I sure was in for a surprise.

The induction never happened because my labor started on its own exactly on my due date. At first, everything went as planned. I labored at home from about seven in the evening until five the next morning. It was difficult but manageable. When the contractions were getting more intense and closer together, we drove to the hospital, checked in, and everything was great. I mean, as great as an active labor can be. We lucked out with a private room overlooking the Hollywood Hills that was a lot nicer than many hotel rooms I'd stayed in over the years. I was already seven centimeters dilated, but the pain was still tolerable, and I was able to laugh with Grant in between contractions. We had our playlist on, I had my game face on, and I was ready to go.

My doctor asked if I wanted an epidural and told me that if I thought I'd want it at any point during the labor, this was the time to do it, so I said yes. Once the epidural kicked in, I took a long nap, during which my doctor apparently also put me on Pitocin, a drug that can induce or speed up labor. There was really no reason to put me on Pitocin, especially without my knowledge, since the labor was progressing normally on its own. I found out later that my doctor had four or five active labors going at once, so the medical team was trying to manage the timing. But it didn't quite work out the way they'd planned.

By seven o'clock that evening, I had been in labor for twenty-four hours when my doctor came in and suddenly said that it was time to start pushing. I didn't feel ready at all. Usually, they temper down the epidural so you can feel enough sensations to know when it's time to push, but I was still 100 percent numb. I was also exhausted, but I was motivated to end the labor and, of course, to meet my baby, so I bore down with all my might and pushed her out in ten pushes.

It felt surreal. I was so numb and out of it that I couldn't feel anything when the baby came out. I didn't even know she had been born until the doctor put her on my chest, and suddenly my entire body flooded with relief. I cried big gulping sobs as I looked into her eyes and took in her squirmy, tiny, perfect newborn body.

That's when things got weird. The room was starting to get dark, and it felt like I was dreaming. A new doctor came in to give me a bigger dose of the epidural medication, and he turned out to be someone Grant had golfed with. That was strange enough, but I also had no idea why they were giving me more meds now, after the baby was born.

So many things were happening to me without my consent or even my understanding. I barely noticed and didn't have the wherewithal to ask any questions because my heart was racing and my mind was so foggy. A nurse brought me a syrupy sweet drink while a whole team of doctors and residents came in. Suddenly, I heard Grant's golfing buddy turn to another doctor and say, "Her blood pressure is dropping. If you give her any more meds, she's going to stop breathing."

It was all a blur. At some point, someone told me that

my placenta wasn't passing normally. It was stuck inside me, so the doctor had to reach in and fish it out. That felt exactly as horrible as it sounds. An entire adult-sized arm was reaching around inside me, and it felt like I was being torn apart.

Once the placenta was out, the doctors said they were going to stitch me up. "Oh, did I tear?" I asked, still clueless. "How bad is it?"

They assured me that the tear wasn't that bad. I should have known better, because it took nearly half an hour for them to finish sewing me up before they wheeled me into a postdelivery room. I don't even know where the baby was at that point. I was still so out of it, and they had taken me off all pain medications because of my drop in blood pressure. Everything seemed fine, though, so once we settled into the new room, Grant ran out to get us both some food. But within the short amount of time in between him leaving and coming back, everything changed.

I was suddenly hit with the most intense, acute pain I have ever felt in my entire life. It felt like someone had sliced me open with a knife. The pain was coming from deep inside me, and with no clue what was causing it, I was convinced that something was horribly wrong. I called Grant and begged him to come back. When he saw how much pain I was in, he was terrified.

Grant is normally quiet and reserved, but he really stepped up. He kept asking to see the doctor and for something to help with the pain. But hours went by, and we were left on our own. I was hysterical, desperate for relief from the pain and to find out what was causing it. I was sure that I was dying and that my precious new baby would grow up without ever having a chance to know her mother.

Finally, a nurse came in and gave me Tylenol. It was so ridiculous that it was almost funny. Tylenol? The over-the-counter drug that you take for a headache? It felt like my insides were ripping apart at the seams. I was scream-ing in pain like I'd never screamed before, not even dur-ing the strongest contractions. Yet no one besides Grant seemed the least bit concerned. The nurses and doctors all seemed to write it off as me having a low pain tolerance, as if these were all normal postpartum pains. Eventually, Grant told the doctors that if they didn't do something about the pain, he was going to go out and find me the drugs I needed on the street.

Finally, at 6:00 a.m., nearly twelve hours after the birth, my doctor came in, checked my stitches, and gave me morphine for the pain. No one had bothered to explain to me that they were concerned about giving me morphine earlier because of my low blood pressure. I heard her and another doctor debating over whether it was a third- or fourth-degree tear. "I don't want to do that to her," she said when they raised the possibility of labeling it as fourth degree. So, it was officially marked as a third-degree tear, which meant it extended into the surrounding muscles. Later, I learned that if they had labeled it as fourth degree, I would have been required to get reconstructive surgery.

We stayed in the hospital for three days while I recov-ered. Grant and I had gone around in circles over what to name our daughter and finally decided on June. The only reason we were still hesitant was because I wanted the name to have a symbolic meaning or a tie to our families. We finally ended up letting Polly choose by putting three names on pieces of paper and a slice of cheese on top of each one. Polly chose June.

When Grant's parents came to the hospital to meet her for the first time, we shared her name: June Marion Leavitt. "Huh." Grant's dad shrugged in a nonchalant way. "June? That was my grandmother's name."

After three days, I was desperate for the comforts of home, but also terrified of going off the morphine and feeling that pain again. Even with the morphine, I could still feel it, just to a lesser degree. They weaned me off it and I was released. Even in my state—I couldn't walk and was a physical and emotional mess—the morning we left the hospital with June, I felt pressured to put a cute outfit on her or at least a pair of Dior booties and get an Instagram-worthy picture. We had naively packed all those things before the birth, not knowing what sort of shape I would be in.

There were competing voices in my head. One said, *Jacey, just be in this moment and live your life. Don't worry about what it looks like.* The other voice constantly pressured me to post and share. It was so ingrained in me at that point. Sharing my life on social media was what Grant and I now did for a living. That voice said, *This is your job. You worked so hard to get here. Keep fighting for your spot, and don't let your readers go away.* That voice was loud, but I couldn't muster the strength to worry about taking a perfect image to post on Instagram. Part of me felt like a failure, but the new me didn't identify with those feelings or let them overtake me.

It's normal for all of us to feel self-doubt. How we process those feelings makes all the difference.

Grant and I had talked in circles about whether or not we wanted to introduce our daughter to the world of social media. At the time, we settled on the idea that we would share very few images of her, as long as it felt safe to do so. I shared the news of June's birth by posting an image of Grant and me during the labor when I had thrown a fist up in the air as if we had just won a gold medal. It put a pretty sheen on an incredibly difficult few days, but more than anything, I was leaving that hospital feeling like I *had* won, because I was going home with June.

I spent the next two weeks at home in bed. Besides the tear, I had somehow fractured my tailbone during the labor and birth, and could barely walk. I had no choice but to stay in bed and let my body heal. Grant was amazing. He handled most of the diaper changes and baby soothing and brought June to me for feedings.

I was breastfeeding and producing milk, but every time I nursed June, I suddenly felt incredibly nauseous, like I was riding a roller coaster blindfolded. I often ended up vomiting and then had to lie down for thirty minutes with my eyes closed, waiting for the nausea to subside. Eight or more times a day, I went through this process of nursing, nausea, vomiting, and then recovering from the whole experience. Then it was time to do it all again! I didn't know what was happening, and because women don't typically talk about these things openly, I had no idea whether or not it was normal.

We had a lactation consultant come to the house, who

told me that I was suffering from a real medical condition called D-MER, Dysphoric Milk Ejection Reflex. D-MER causes levels of dopamine, a neurotransmitter that helps stabilize mood, to drop more quickly than usual when a mother starts nursing. Normally, dopamine levels drop gradually to allow prolactin, the hormone that causes milk to be released, to rise. This quick drop in dopamine can lead to a host of physical and mental symptoms. For me, it manifested in extreme nausea and vomiting every time I tried to nurse.

Like so many women's health issues, there has been very little research or attention dedicated to D-MER. The lactation consultant basically told me to suck it up. But I was suffering, and I knew there was no way I could keep this up long-term and function in any sort of reasonable way.

It was a difficult and emotional decision to give up breastfeeding. I felt like my body was failing me, and it was causing me to be unable to provide for my daughter. But the second I quit, it felt like a huge weight had been lifted from me. I could finally rest, and I immediately took a big step forward in my recovery.

Just a few days later, I was already feeling so much better. I was able to get up and take a shower, and with the warm water beating down on me, I could tell that I was still producing milk. I decided to try to nurse June one more time, before it was too late and my milk was gone for good.

I lifted June from her bassinet and sat down in the tan rocking chair I had gotten from Monte. She began to nurse, and I smiled, looking down at her perfect little face. How had I created that? For a minute, everything felt okay. Maybe I had gotten past the D-MER and would be able to do this. Then, just as suddenly as before, the room started spinning around me. I barely had enough time to put June safely back in her bassinet and run to the bathroom to throw up.

I had no more guilt about not breastfeeding after that. That is, until I went to my checkup and the doctor asked whether I was breastfeeding or pumping. I felt defensive for those of us who couldn't breastfeed and snapped back, "Umm...neither."

On Instagram, I saw dozens of my fellow moms sharing images of themselves proudly breastfeeding. I was happy for them. But I was one of the unlucky ones who couldn't proudly display what I was feeding my newborn: some fancy European formula called HiPP. I never felt guilty for my choices in my own bubble and my own life, but sometimes society and social media made me feel differently.

After I stopped breastfeeding, I started feeling better physically, but mentally and emotionally, I felt like I'd been dropped on another planet. My postpartum hormones were just as difficult as they were during pregnancy, plus now I somehow had to show up every day as a mom. I didn't know what I was doing. My postpartum hormones amplified my ADHD, and I obsessed over tracking feeding and naps and diaper changes because I was so forgetful. But none of my typical controlling, researching, perfectionist coping mechanisms worked. I just had to survive day by day at the mercy of this brand-new human.

All new parents go through this, but I didn't handle it

particularly well. Underscoring every miraculous moment with June, of which there were many, was the pressure to recover, bounce back, and be able to perform at my job. In the mornings, Grant and I would lie in bed with June and swoon over her perfect fingers and toes and eyelashes. It was so wild that we had created her out of nothing! Then, flooded with feelings of love and happiness, I would go get dressed and land with a thump back in reality, where I was still twenty-five pounds above my normal weight and my once toned and athletic body could barely tolerate a short walk.

At my six-week postpartum checkup, my doctor pronounced me ready to have sex, work out, and go back to life as normal, but I felt nowhere near ready to do any of those things. Inside my own body and my own life, I was a foreigner. Nothing was remotely similar to how it was before or even recognizable. And once again, I made things so much worse by beating myself up, this time for not being able to bounce back. My inner voice constantly berated me, saying that I was fat and ugly and a horrible mom.

My ADHD and anxiety spiraled around each other, each one making the other worse. I started having panic attacks over whether or not my HiPP formula was the right food for June and stayed up until 2:00 a.m., researching on my phone about any tiny issue she was having, such as reflux or a slight rash.

When I finally started to wind down in the middle of the night, I walked those twenty-three steps to the bathroom and stopped at a pocket window to stare out at the city lights. A stray cat typically strutted by, causing our backyard motion sensor light to go off. And almost every night, I saw a figure dressed all in white, wearing a hat and a long trench coat. He was leaning up against the studio office next to our rose garden. As I made my way to the bathroom, I could shrug off the ghost as a figment of my imagination, but then as I got back in bed I had visions of June with a blue face, lying in a puddle of water. Just as my heavy, sleepy eyelids fell, I jumped out of bed after seeing an image of her being hit by a car.

These images seemed so real, and they were terrifying. I told myself that, of course, I was anxious. What new mother wasn't? I had a new living, breathing human to take care of, one that was more precious to me than anything in this world. But I knew it was more than just typical "new mom" anxiety when I started having images of throwing myself down the stairs, and thought to myself, *That would be such a relief.* This feeling lasted for a while. I didn't want to kill myself. I was sure of that. But the idea of hurting myself and landing back in the hospital was sickly appealing.

I was still trying to control everything—June's sleeping and eating schedule, what she wore, and how she acted. If I dressed her in a perfect outfit with bows to try to get a picture, she'd immediately spit up all over it, and I caught myself feeling resentful. I had always been scared of letting go. I gripped the wheel tightly so things didn't spiral out of control. But now, no matter how hard I gripped, I couldn't force things to go my way.

I realize now that I was obviously struggling with a form of postpartum depression. I was honest with Grant about how I was feeling, and of course our main focus was on keeping June safe. I would never ever have hurt her on purpose. But one day I hit a new low and screamed so loudly the neighbors came by to check on us.

Grant took June away from me while I punched the wall and screamed at the top of my lungs with rage. The neighbors rang our doorbell several times, but I could not hear it over my rage. It wasn't until the ADT patrol officer stopped by the house that I realized how disruptive and unhealthy my behavior truly was. I knew that I needed the tools to course correct very quickly.

Grant and I developed a code word that I could use anytime I needed a time-out. When I said that word, he would swoop in and take care of June so I could go take some breaths and calm myself down. My therapist also recommended getting my energy out physically by focusing all my emotions and every ounce of strength on pushing up against a wall as hard as I could. It sounds strange, but it really helped release that pressure valve in my system. Then I would go for a walk by myself. Like many new parents, Grant and I were in the house all day with June, just trying to stay afloat between naps and feedings and spit-up and diaper changes, but Grant noticed that I was a different person when I got dressed and left the house each day. It stabilized me, while staying home left me feeling trapped and ready to explode.

It took months, but as my moods and hormones finally started to balance out with the help of these tools, I was slowly able to accept the fact that I was never going to be a perfect mom. I wasn't posting much during this time, just pictures of June here and there and the content I had shot early in my pregnancy. I didn't want anyone to look at my feed and expect new parenthood to be easy. It was important to me to post honestly about what it was like to parent June.

I didn't just owe it to myself or my readers, but I owed it to my daughter. What kind of example would I be setting if I went back to living a filtered life on and off social media? I wanted her and everyone else following our lives to know that it was okay for things to look and feel a bit sloppy at times. I had learned that being imperfect was okay. Now it was time to show it and lead by example.

At first, I made the shift visually, by sharing selfies and raw images and nothing that looked glossy or staged or was in any way sugarcoated. Later, I added more and more content that matched this new level of honesty. It was tough to know how much of June to share with my followers. Every time I posted a picture of her, they asked for more. They told me that it brought them joy to see her little face, and I understood this. Especially before becoming a mom, I loved when the bloggers I followed shared pics of their kids. It felt innocent and joyful in a world that was otherwise superficial and competitive, and of course I wanted to share that with my followers.

It also would have felt strange and unnatural for me not to share pictures of June. Social media was our family business now. Of course she was going to be a part of it. But how big of a part? This is a question that Grant and I have asked ourselves and each other, and as she grows up we'll keep asking and reasking.

My followers also told me that when I shared June, it helped them see a new side of me. In fact, many of them admitted that they had never really liked me before I became a mom. *Humph.* Maybe they'd appreciated my style or my writing, but they never liked me as a person. Now they saw that I was actually human (imagine that!), and they felt connected to me in a different way. Although I still wasn't getting new work for the first few months after June was born, I hoped this would eventually translate to the industry as a whole, and that brands would also see potential in this new side of me.

To kick this off, I scheduled a trip to New York for me, June, and Grant when June was four months old to meet with brands, remind them that I still existed, and let them see this new version of me as a working mom. Traveling with a newborn was a whole new experience!

When we finally walked into our room at the Four Seasons with our luggage, our stroller, Polly, and June, I saw a vase of peonies in the center of the table. "Oh, I wonder who these are from," I said merrily as I crossed the room. I opened the card. "Welcome back," it read. "From the Housekeeping Staff." I burst out laughing, remembering how upset I'd been the first time I'd received flowers from the staff instead of from Grant. Now Grant was with me in every way. I didn't need flowers to prove it. I put the card down. "They probably leave these for every guest."

I stacked my days in New York with meetings, which went well, but I could still sense hesitance on the part of some brands to work with me so soon after having a baby. I knew I could win them back over, but that it might take time. Apparently, even many years of networking did not supersede questions about whether or not I would return to work after having June. For a moment, I wondered if they would have asked Grant the same questions if he were taking those meetings without me.

From New York, we flew to Turks and Caicos to shoot some content for the Aman, an amazing resort on a huge nature reserve. I was grateful for that gig to help keep us afloat until other brands came around. The island and the resort were beautiful, and the content we shot there performed really well. But having to shoot myself on the beach four months postpartum was a challenge. My body was nothing like it was before my pregnancy, and I was not in a good place with my confidence.

Logically, I knew there was no reason to expect my body to ever go back to the way it was before, not now and maybe not ever. The point was to move forward, not backward. I knew that, and I was trying to give myself some grace and compassion as I slowly worked to get into a new shape that I felt good about. But I just didn't feel my best being photographed in a bathing suit at the time, especially knowing that no matter what I looked like, my body would be probably picked apart online. It took a lot of time to fully accept my post-baby body. It still doesn't look or feel the same as it did before I had June, but I work out and do yoga regularly, I feel strong and healthy, and I am happy with myself as I am.

Looking back at pictures of myself from this time, you can see my insecurities reflected in my clothes. Instead of the colors and patterns and layers and accessories that

I normally wore, I covered up in plain-Jane sweaters and jeans. I wasn't sure what I wanted my outfits to say about who I was. Was I just a mom now and meant to dress dowdily, or was I still young and hot? What even existed in between those two extremes? I had this idea that moms could only dress one way, but that image of a mom in gray sweaters with her knees always covered didn't feel like me at all. At the same time, I felt uneasy in my own skin and wasn't ready to wear anything skimpy or that called attention to me.

Back in LA, I was in the little seating area off our bathroom, which we called the pamper room. It was sunny and pink and felt like the brightest and happiest room in our house. It was one of those hectic days that are the norm with a baby. The nap didn't go as planned and the whole day was thrown into chaos.

Whenever June napped, I desperately tried to squeeze in either some work or a workout. This day, I finally got June down and went into the pamper room and put on a workout video. Just a few minutes in, the cheerful, skinny girl in the video told us to hold a plank, and I just couldn't do it. I wasn't strong enough. Before my pregnancy, I could have held a plank for days. At least, that's how I remembered it. But now I felt weak and exhausted and honestly just worthless.

This was my rock-bottom moment, at least as far as my post-pregnancy body image was concerned. I sat there on the floor, crying. I had been trying to work out as much as possible and watch what I ate, and nothing was really moving the needle.

People think rock bottom is a terrible place to be, and it is. But it's also incredibly liberating to know that you've sunken to your lowest point and have nowhere to go but up. It's a cliché for a reason. In that moment, I knew that I had to accept my body as it was, stop fighting with myself, and figure out how to breathe through these moments instead of attaching to them. My body had created and birthed June. She was a miracle. How could there be anything wrong with the body that had carried her for nine months and given her life?

Once I stopped crying, I wrote a new blog post straight from my heart about how much I was struggling and that, quite frankly, I was feeling like crap that day. Within minutes, I had dozens of comments saying that I didn't look like crap, that I was doing great, and that these women had also struggled with all the same issues and more. As I pulled myself off the floor, I realized that I hadn't just built a support system and community for my followers— I had built one for myself.

Before June was born, I had been motivated to keep my life fun and interesting for the sake of my followers. I jumped off the boat into the ice-cold water in Positano to get a cute pic I could post. I ventured out on the rock climb instead of lounging in bed for the same reason. I always said yes to the last-minute trip to a new destination. My followers had motivated me to live a richer and more exciting life. Yes, sometimes this was to a fault, but I had gained so many wonderful moments along the way. And now they were there to pull me out of my funk and help propel me toward an exciting new future.

That summer, when June was six months old, we rented a villa in Italy for five weeks. Let me start by saying that, yes, it was a bit of a stretch to be traveling across the globe with a newborn. I was pushing us hard, but I wanted to keep experiencing those Instagram-worthy moments, not just for the sake of my followers, but so that we could enjoy them as a family, too.

Of course, traveling with a six-month-old was difficult, not to mention the fact that there are zero diaper changing stations in Italian bathrooms, but we had so many great moments on that trip: eating ice cream and going to the local market and making huge dinners in the tiny kitchen with a big farm table that acted as an island. We frequented the local market, became addicted to mortadella, and drank wine like it was water.

During the day, we tried to spend as much time as possible by the pool out back that overlooked the picturesque hills of Tuscany. I was still twenty pounds above my pre-baby weight, but I gave myself a break from dieting while we were there and enjoyed all the pasta and pizza and gelato that I wanted. I wasn't going to let the pressure to fit into sample sizes keep me from fully experiencing this trip.

We did some work while we were in Italy. I felt a bit hesitant at first about one campaign, with the eco-friendly and size-inclusive swimsuit brand Summersalt, but their bathing suits were so comfortable and flattering that when I was wearing them I felt more at home in my skin than I had in a long time. I was wearing one of their one-shouldered one-pieces in red, pink, and white with a white caftan thrown on top when Grant snapped a pic of me dipping my foot into the pool with the Tuscan countryside spectacularly displayed behind me. Our deal with Summersalt was supposed to be a one-off, but that photo performed so well that the brand asked us to keep doing more. I loved working with the team at Summersalt, and eventually I agreed to design a capsule collection for them.

This deal with Summersalt is what put us back on the map, professionally and financially. It was no coincidence that this happened just as I was managing to let go of my body-image issues and come out of my postpartum fog. The Summersalt brand is known for their inclusive sizing and empowering messaging. It was the perfect brand to align myself with after my postpartum journey.

As I started to feel more comfortable in my body and as a new mom, it showed in what I wore. This was intentional. I imagined a role model for myself—a strong, sexy, powerful married woman and mother. That was who I wanted to be, and I modeled my outfits after what I pictured her wearing.

Each morning, instead of asking myself what would look good on Instagram, I chose what would make me feel like that woman (and therefore my true self) during the day. This often meant shedding layers, accessorizing boldly, and going back to classic styles, like a white button-down with skinny trousers.

In a way, I was getting back to the whole reason I had started the blog to begin with—to help women feel confident and empowered, like the role model I held up for myself instead of the damsel in distress I had too often felt myself to be. Who was that role model? Of course, she was a Damsel in Dior. It turns out, she was also me. That's who I was looking for the whole time. I had just been looking in the wrong places. The funny thing is, instead of helping my followers feel more like a Damsel in Dior, that's exactly what they ended up doing for me.

13

Off the Grid

Two Years Later

THERE ARE THOUSANDS OF ROCKS ON THE PATH
from our family home in Concan, Texas, down to the
Frio River. In the ninety-degree July heat, we walked and
stumbled our way, one rock at a time, to take June for her
first dip in the same body of water I learned to swim in
nearly thirty-eight years before.

We were in Texas for the Fourth of July and to celebrate
Meme's ninetieth birthday. She had been battling a chronic
lung condition called bronchiectasis for the past two years
and would need an oxygen tank for the rest of her life.
Normally, she would be walking down to the river with us

and bending down to search for heart-shaped rocks to add to our collection. For the first time, she opted to stay back at the house with a few of my cousins. Thirty members of our extended family had made the trip back to Texas for her birthday, finally able to spend time together in person for the first time in ages.

This was our first trip with June since COVID-19 basically shut down the entire planet. It was fitting that it was a full-circle voyage back to the place of my happiest childhood moments, the same place I had traveled to in my mind the moment I had decided to become a mom. We were emerging from the bubble of quarantine cautiously, like baby birds peeping their heads out of their eggs. The past year and a half had been difficult, of course, on so many levels. But being grounded and forced to stay still for so long brought a new emotion for me that I was determined to hang on to, and that was a feeling of contentment, of peace.

The year 2020 had started out great for us. Work was very slowly starting to pick back up after my pregnancy and June's birth, although deals certainly weren't coming through at nearly the same rate as before. I was thinking about doing something to up the ante and push the brand to be more than just a fashion blog when we stumbled upon a pop-up shop at a nearby outdoor mall. Unlike The Grove, another popular outdoor shopping center in LA with the kind of chain stores you can find at every mall throughout the country, this one, Platform, had a hipster vibe and unique, edgy stores that Grant and I loved.

I had never really thought about opening my own store,

but the idea of creating a short-term pop-up that carried my favorite brands sounded exciting and fun. It was something that no other bloggers had really done, and I knew how to sell products, both online and IRL. A project like this would help us stand out, and most important, the idea inspired me. If deals weren't coming to me the way they used to, I could fill that void by creating something myself. This helped me feel powerful and in control of my destiny instead of feeling like I was at the mercy of brands to decide whether or not they wanted to work with me.

I put together a beautifully designed application for a pop-up shop called By Damsel that would carry items that were each hand-selected by me. We would not only sell clothes, of course, but the entire store would also be shoppable, from the wallpaper to the furniture to the clothes on display. My application was accepted, and I threw myself completely into creating an amazing experience for shoppers.

Despite the techniques I had learned to breathe through tough moments instead of attaching to toxic thoughts, when I was at home with June, "new mom" anxiety still sometimes ate away at me. A simple case of diaper rash or baby acne would send me down a rabbit hole of research as my ADHD took over and I obsessed over potential cures and deadly diseases that could be at the root of these common symptoms. Having a creative, healthy outlet to direct all that energy toward helped me enjoy my time with June instead of obsessing.

For the store, I wanted to create an immersive, full sensory experience for shoppers. I made a playlist of hipster oldies and current hits to create a fresh but relatable vibe. I reached out to Santa Maria Novella, the oldest pharmacy in Florence, which we had visited on our trip to Italy the summer before. They sell fragrances and had the exact scent I wanted for the space. I sourced clothes with a specific tactile feel, like the soft cotton T-shirts and jeans from AMO Denim and cashmere knits from FILORO. Then I layered this with vintage furniture, locally made jewelry, homemade ceramics designed by one of our close friends, and photographs from another online friend that weren't available for sale anywhere else. The result was a physical space that was my entire blog come to life.

While I focused more on the creative side, Grant became the store manager, dealing with hiring and all that came with it. He was fully in charge of HR, payroll, accounting, and acting as a liaison between the Platform staff and our company. He organized store events, dealt with vendors, and kept a close eye on tracking our sales and inventory. It was a full-time job on top of his full-time job at Damsel Inc.

On opening day, I was nervous. It was one thing to read my blog or follow me on Instagram, but would that translate to people wanting to shop in a space I had created? I stood in the empty store, nervously running my hands over the merchandise and rearranging every item so that everything was absolutely perfect. The store had floor-to-ceiling windows that faced the Platform courtyard, and we had wallpapered the opposite wall using a sea-toned blue print from House of Hackney. It had white birds and beautiful olive branch leaves, which made the space feel eclectic. The racks were attached to the wall, and rather than having all our inventory on the floor, I carefully curated a small selection of pieces and shuffled brands among one another to showcase how to mix and match designers.

We quietly opened our doors. I didn't announce opening day on my Instagram, nor did we have a big store-opening event. I was too nervous that we wouldn't be ready and wanted a chance to work out any kinks in the system. Finally, a couple of young women came in. I wanted to rush over and see how I could help them, but suddenly everything I'd learned from working at Celeste's as a salesgirl came back to me, and I remembered to hang back and approach them in a friendly, nonaggressive way.

After they'd browsed quietly for a few minutes, I smiled at them. "Do you guys watch *The Good Place*?" I asked the one woman who was standing closer to me. "You remind me so much of Tahani."

"Oh, thank you," she said, pulling a red Heidi Merrick dress from the rack. "That's such a compliment. I've been following you for years." We chatted for a few minutes, and then she told me that she was looking for something to wear to a friend's upcoming wedding. "What do you think of this dress?"

"Hmm." I walked across the store to another rack that held Clare V., Hunting Season, and Lunya. "That would look great on you, but I think this maroon one might work even better." I held up a LACAUSA dress, and her face lit up. "Try it with these earrings," I said, grabbing a wooden pair from Sophie Monet, a local designer from Venice Beach.

Over the next twenty minutes, I helped her pick out a bag and sold her on a fifteen-hundred-dollar necklace from Retrouvai, and she left with an entire wedding outfit that she felt great in. It made me so happy to know that in a small way, I had played a role in helping her feel joyful and confident at her friend's wedding. Meanwhile, her friend selected a few products from Santa Maria Novella to give to her mom for the upcoming holidays. It was just as rewarding to know that this woman I had never met would receive a special gift.

That night, Celeste flew in to surprise me and see the store. I was so touched, and having Celeste there with me felt like a beautiful full-circle moment. I had put everything I'd learned from her to work in that store, and I took her for a tour, showing her how I had hung everything just the way she had back at Celeste's.

Celeste's opinion had always carried a lot of weight for me, and when she said that I had done a good job, it was one of the proudest moments of my career. Soon after, *Vogue* ran a piece, featuring the store. It was one of the final items on the bucket list I had naively created in my Moleskine journal so many years before.

I felt validated, accepted, respected, and most of all, "en vogue." That was all I'd ever wanted. But helping people by sharing the things I was passionate about was more rewarding than any external validation.

It was the exact opposite of how I had felt back when my family visited me on the set of *The Oprah Winfrey Show*. Back then, I was so focused on what other people thought of me and desperate to win a gold star for my performance that I had made the wrong wishes and chased the wrong goals. Of course, it felt empty when I got what I thought I'd wanted. I was going after things that didn't truly fulfill me. Now, receiving praise for a job well done felt nice, but it was just the cherry on top of a sundae made of passion and purpose and true meaning. It wasn't the sundae itself.

June was still a baby and required a ton of our time and attention, but having the store nearby allowed Grant and me to go back and forth as needed. Lucky for us, my mom had moved to LA shortly after June was born to spend as much time with her granddaughter as possible. It felt amazing to be working at the store during the day, interacting with my audience again, and selling products one-on-one. I was clawing my way out of my "pregnancy and new mom" hole and getting back to myself.

I also saw, perhaps for the first time, that I could do things that made me happy and stay relevant and interesting in this industry without jet-setting to five countries a week or participating in drama and competition among my peers. I could just do what I loved and share that with the amazing community I had created. Looking at it that way, there was no limit to what Grant and I could do together.

I loved having the store, but it was always intended to be a short-term pop-up. After our two-month lease was up, work on the blog really started to pick up. We had a good sales record with Amazon after our first deal with them, and landed an Ambassador deal, which meant multiple posts per month on my various social media channels and blog, as well as designing a full collection. It felt like Damsel Inc. was finally fully back. We had our calendar for the entire year meticulously planned out to maximize our content and productivity, and we were off and running.

Then COVID hit. Like everyone else, at first I thought (or hoped) the lockdowns would only last for a few weeks. I threw myself into "Netflix and Chill" mode, encouraging my followers to stay at home and get cozy. I was determined to still get dressed every day as a way of holding on to some small piece of normalcy, and I continued to post on the blog about work-from-home fashion, ingredients for at-home facials, and recipes for at-home cocktail hours.

But with the entire world suddenly turned upside down, it was a hard balance to strike. If I posted frivolous content in the midst of a pandemic, would people think I was ignoring the suffering that was going on around me? I didn't want to pretend that everything was hunky-dory, but I didn't want the blog to become a source of doom and gloom, either. If people were coming to my channels, I wanted them to find some relief there, an escape from the darkness that surrounded them.

Ultimately, I had to ask myself some hard questions. What was the true role of my blog? In the midst of a global pandemic, was it completely frivolous and vapid? Did the clothes I was wearing really matter?

As the lockdowns wore on and I gave in to the sweats and athleisure outfits that everyone was simultaneously embracing, the answer I found was yes and no. Of course, there were far more important things in the world than fashion and labels, especially during this time, but on some level, what I wore did matter because it impacted how I felt. This was, of course, the original philosophy behind

Damsel in Dior, yet the blog had gone through many figurative and literal outfit changes over the years.

Ironically, I came home to this original viewpoint in lockdown because there was no one around for me to dress for or to try to impress besides me. My clothes didn't have to be an armor that I used to face the world because, for better or worse, I wasn't facing the world. I was just facing myself in the mirror every day. It was past time for me to start dressing for the woman I saw there instead of creating a facade, trying to please others or living up to some imaginary ideal.

Every day, I decided to wear whatever made me feel the most comfortable and happy. Getting dressed became easy and stress-free. By then, my wardrobe consisted mostly of classic pieces that could easily be paired together. A loose-fitting pair of faded denim that gave at the knees so I could kneel down easily and hug June. A white cotton tank from Splendid that was perfectly fitted so I didn't need to wear a bra underneath. A light tan blazer from J.Crew that I'd owned for five years, with pockets that held my Carmex lip balm and my cell phone. A discontinued pair of chunky black Celine sandals. A simple cotton tote bag that felt special and personal because Dior had gifted it to me along with an invite to one of their shows. My promise ring from Grant on my finger, always reminding me of what really matters.

Each of these items meant something to me and said something about who I was: a mom, a small-business owner, a wife, a fashionista, and a farmer's daughter. They didn't create a persona or a facade. Instead, they revealed the pieces of my identity that finally blended together as seamlessly as the wardrobe staples I'd spent my life coveting. Yes, my clothes mattered because they made me feel like me, like Jacey, in all my imperfect glory, and because they told the world who I really was. But, no, they did not define me.

My plan for the year had seemed great on paper, but now that I had experienced the exact opposite, I realized that all that travel wasn't what I had really wanted. If our year had gone as planned, we would have missed out on precious moments like seeing June start to really take off walking, learning to talk, eating solid foods, and kissing Polly on the cheek.

During lockdown, there were days when it felt like nothing happened at all and the walls were closing in on us. Then there were days that the smallest moment, such as June saying, "I wuv you, Mommy," turned it into the biggest, most important day of my life.

Like so many people experienced, COVID woke me up to what truly mattered. It put a magnifying glass over my daily decisions, and I saw that I had not been using my time with intention. I didn't want to be far away from June so often, filling my schedule every day with things that were unimportant compared to my family. I loved my work and the community I had created, and it would always be an important part of my life. But it wasn't my entire life, and I would never be whole if I tried to find fulfillment in a job that could never really love me back.

It became a daily practice for me to focus first and foremost on the things that meant the most to me, June and

Grant, and draw a boundary around everything else. I became extremely focused on living in the present and picked up habits like always taking three deep breaths before getting into my car. The blog would still be there after I rocked June to sleep, after I spent time connecting with Grant, and even after I took some time to take care of myself. I had started the blog to help people feel confident, and I couldn't do that unless I felt good about my world, my choices, and myself.

The year of COVID slowed down time tremendously and gave me the gift of slowing down my time with June as well. The moment I was able to let go of my past, let go of control, practice breathing, and find my ground was the moment I was able to be fully present and responsible as a parent to June. It didn't take one or two or three moments where I was fully engulfed in playing hide-and-seek or singing "Let It Go." It took all the tiny slivers of time in between that added up, creating real happiness.

Before having June, I was afraid to have a child. I realize now that I wasn't really worried about exhaustion or the ways in which my life would change. I was scared because I didn't want to mess it up. I was scared because I saw motherhood as the greatest emotional challenge and inner battle that I would ever face, and I didn't know if I could do it.

For a long time, those fears held me back from so much goodness that life has to offer. June taught me the second she was born that we are all born in love. My only hope is that, in return, I can show her to always have the courage to trust and believe in herself, and know deep within her heart that during tough times, I will always be in her corner.

I hope this knowledge gives her the confidence to always be true to herself, to love herself with wild abandon, to grow so incredibly comfortable in her own skin and with her own needs and her own true desires that she isn't concerned with what other people think of her. I want her to never ever feel like a damsel in distress and to know that no matter what she's wearing, she has the inner strength to feel as confident and secure as a Damsel in Dior. I want this for every young girl and woman in this world because that is what we all need and what we deserve.

As the world slowly started to open back up again, I immediately knew the very first trip I wanted to take June on would be back to Texas. Apparently, I wasn't the only one craving family time, because on July Fourth weekend, thirty of our family members on my mom's side traveled to Concan to be together.

Once we were close to the river, we joined my parents and my brother, Justin, his husband, Josh, and their son, Finn. At that point, I had posted very little on Instagram about the trip because I was too busy managing June on the plane and getting settled into the cabin we had rented across the street from our family house. I had been looking forward to this trip all year.

I dressed June in an adorable new checkered swimsuit I'd gotten just for the trip, and to my surprise, I had a similarly colored suit that matched hers. It was a happy coincidence that we were twinning, but I didn't rush to snap a pic. How many more years did I have before June started hating the idea of matching her mom?

The closer we got to the river, the more June's excitement began to rise. She took off toward the water with Finn following close behind. Grant and Josh swam with the kids while my mom, dad, Justin, and I sat on the rocks along the river, watching the two cousins splash and scream.

In addition to Meme's birthday and the Fourth of July, we were also celebrating my dad's fifteenth anniversary of sobriety. What had seemed impossible for so long had actually happened, and through his own hard work and commitment, he'd managed to stay sober for fifteen years. Even more miraculous, we had grown so close by then that we called each other daily, and outside of COVID lockdown, he made monthly trips out to Los Angeles to see the grandkids.

My dad often said that he wished he could take back the years he had wasted drinking, but I was thankful for all of it. Our relationship had become one of the closest bonds I've ever shared with anyone. I could tell him anything with no judgment, and he was always, always there with an open mind and an open heart. Who knows if that would have been possible if we hadn't gone through every step of our journey?

Despite it all—or because of it all—there we sat as a family, talking about weather patterns, just like the stars in the sky. "You know, it's so crazy how these rocks came back to the way they were when you guys were kids," my dad said. "There are so many floods and intense thunderstorms, tropical depressions, and effects from hurricanes in the gulf that cause these rocks to shift, move, and reshape the edge of the river. One more rain or flood and they'll be in an entirely different place."

My dad picked up a small rock, holding it in between his fingers. "I wonder how far this rock has traveled to be in this exact place at this exact time," he mused. "And who knows where it will end up next?"

Home is always home, no matter where you are or what surrounds you.

For my entire life, I have been moving, shifting, and reshaping myself, just like those rocks. Like my dad, I had traveled far to end up back here, and for a while, I didn't know where I was headed. I was fighting against nature, lost, allowing intense storms and depressions to toss me wildly in midair. But now that I had let go of the reins, I was right back to where I was supposed to be. That didn't mean I'd start standing still. Moving makes room for growth, for evolution, for the impossible to become possible. But I was flowing with the river, instead of fighting the current.

I looked out at June and smiled just seeing how happy she looked in the water.

"Grant," I called out. "Will you take our picture?" I jumped up and splashed into the water with June, feeling the rocks under my feet while Grant snapped a few photos of us in our matching swimsuits. We were smiling ear to ear, and I felt filled with joy from having my family all together, swimming in the river.

Sometimes the best moments happen off the Instagram

grid, but sometimes they happen on it. Over the past ten years of working as a social media influencer and sharing my life online, the filters and boundaries I have set for myself have varied as much from season to season as the wildest labels' looks. But now, what I chose to share, what I chose to wear, and when and how I shared these things were choices I felt confident making.

I looked around me, soaking it all in. My mom was taking a video of her grandchildren. My dad was fifteen years sober. My brother and his family splashed nearby. And Grant, my rock, was acting like a typical dad, proudly taking photos of his family on vacation.

I left the photo of June and me unfiltered, and posted it to my grid.

★ ★ ★ ★ ★

Acknowledgments

Dad, for always telling me that I have creativity, a powerful intuition, and magic within me since the day I was born. You showed me the stars. I didn't get to share the man in Italy story, the beautiful poem you wrote about the treasure of Forrest Fenn, or the amazing memories we've shared together riding tractors, on our daily phone calls, and on trips to Italy. But as you say, I must save something for my next book. Thank you for teaching me that it's okay to be human. Thank you for telling me to write it all and for always believing in me that I am a writer. Thank you for letting me share your rock-bottom moments and still telling me that you loved reading it. Thank you for showing me that you are proud of me just by the way you look at me. I love our laughs. We will always be searching for treasure, for the northern lights, and for gold in the reefs of Cozumel.

Mom, for not only giving me life, but showing me how to live it with love, compassion, and confidence. I would have never had the courage to follow my dreams without you in my corner. Whether it's singing in the car to The Judds or laughing about tiki torches, you will always be my best friend. Thank you for being so strong for us and for being the best mom I could ask for. I'm not easy. You have done an incredible job at being our mom.

Justin, my brother and first friend in life. Thank you for teaching me about the wonderful world of make-believe. It seems simple, but you have always met my imagination and curiosity down the rabbit hole, and you always held my hand when I wanted to go there. I love you and Josh and Finn, always.

Grant, what a lovely table, so close to the buffet. I will never be able to adequately thank you for your constant support, love, and patience. Thank you for making me laugh through it all and being a true partner in life. Thank you for every read, every edit, every late-night talk, and every time I wake you up in the middle of the night thinking I "heard something." Thank you for not giving up, even when I thought I wanted to. You've seen me at my lowest, you've seen me at my highest, and you've loved me relentlessly and unconditionally. "Never more than today."

June, for showing me my own strength and reminding me to play, smile, and be kind every day. You will always be my northern light.

A heartfelt thank-you to the Leavitt family for being my silent but strong support system in my off-screen life.

I wish I could have written more about my incredibly supportive and loving extended family in this book. They have all been my best friends and support system throughout my life. Meme and C.R., Granny and Dutch, Terri, Jenda, Sandy, Celeste, Sue, Uncle Noe, Jim, and Larry, and my dozens of loving and fun cousins. I always knew that I was one of the lucky ones to have such a strong and supportive family. You have all had my back no matter what. You are also the people whom I always wish to have one more minute of time with. Whether it's getting lost searching for heart-shaped rocks in Concan, singing karaoke, exploring Granny's rose garden, or wearing matching tie-dye shirts at Disney World, my best memories are with you, with my family.

★ ★ ★

My deepest, darkest secrets and biggest insecurities lie in the vault of Jodi Lipper. This book would not have been possible without you and your tireless dedication, patience, and passion for my story—our story. The process of writing a book can feel so intimidating, heavy, and at times it felt very difficult to go back and revisit traumatic moments from my past. Thank you for holding my hand through it all and for the edits and revisions and edits and emails and phone calls and texts and phone calls and laughs. I simply cannot thank you enough.

Hilary Williams, my beautiful friend and dedicated manager. You asked me what I wanted, and you made it happen. We did it! You are a wonderful woman to have in my corner.

The best managers in the business work at Digital Brand Architects and United Talent Agency, and I'm so incredibly lucky to have all your support. Raina Penchansky, Vanessa Flaherty, and Reesa Lake, I have always admired your worth ethic and ability to juggle it all so gracefully.

What makes a great agent? Someone who instills faith, trust, confidence, and excitement in a project and their client no matter what. Through multiple revisions, a global pandemic, and so many ups and downs, the cheerful tone of your voice, positive outlook, and constant support truly made this book come to life. Albert Lee, you make the world a better place to be.

Erika, for believing in this project and steering our ship with grace and wisdom. Your trust and patience carried us from our first outline to this final copy, and we couldn't have done it without you. The entire team at Park Row and HarperCollins was such a pleasure to work with on this book. A special thank-you to Rachel Haller, Laura Gianino, Lindsey Reeder, Erin Craig, Alex Niit, and the full force behind Marketing, Publicity, Sales, and Production at Park Row and HarperCollins. Thank you all so, so much for believing in me.

Align PR, for getting this book into the hands of so many people around the world. I'm forever grateful for your dedication and passion for this project.

★ ★ ★

Shannon, for staying up until midnight learning the dance moves to *Thriller*. You somehow make me cry through tears, and while I never had a blood sister, you're the next best thing.

Gia, did you get the peaches? "There are good ships. And wood ships. And ships that sail the sea. But the best ships are friendships. And may they always be."

Ashley, for picking up the phone and inviting me to reunite. I can't imagine my life without you in it as my friend.

Catt/Ruthie, for getting me out of bed at 10:00 p.m. to meet my future husband. For being the kind of friend who continues to enlighten and inspire me daily.

Lina/Boss-Hog, for always making us laugh and building me up. In my less than beautiful moments in life, you always make me feel beautiful.

Haleigh, for being the world's best assistant and an even better friend. Even though you left your assistant role years ago to conquer the world, I'm so lucky to have you in my life.

Erin, who will most likely find a spelling error in this book. You always see the goodness in others, and it has taught me to always look for the good, too.

Felicia Lasala, for loving me through your lens over the past ten years.

Filtering through my complex thoughts and shaded past took a great deal of time, patience, and incredible support. Kathryn Lebow, thank you for your encouragement, guidance, and trust.

Namaste to Joe Komar, who continually inspires and guides me to breathe through it all.

Instagram, you pushed me outside of my comfort zone at times and, most important, introduced me to so many friends and colleagues along the way. My blog was my original expression of creativity and passion, but you gave me the wings to fly.

To my incredible community of readers, followers, and cheerleaders who have been a part of our lives over the years. Thank you for every click, every comment, every email, note, word of encouragement, and for showing up for us with your time, thoughtfulness, and efforts. Our blog, and this book, simply would not have been possible without your support. I cannot thank you enough for being a part of the ride. Also thank you to my fellow bloggers, influencers, and fashion friends for all your incredible support over the years.

These acknowledgments would simply not feel complete without mentioning the jerk economics teacher that I had during my senior year of high school. It's such a cliché that this happened to me. Thank you for telling me that I would never amount to anything. It's been a pleasure proving you wrong.

Finally, a very big thank-you to these special people who have been supportive and a big part of my journey on and off social media: Maria Alonzo, Burke Eiteljorg, Kylee Prusack, Stephanie Soechtig, Joseph Orozco, Kirsty Surian, Isabelle Blye, Hilary Fash, Stefanie Skinner, Scott Wilson, Brian Schall, Heather and Erik Hodge, the Chang-Bars, the Buhais, Amber O'Connell, Jessica Mirschak, Kate Krieger, Nathalie Simon, Sydney Waters, Gaby Dalkin, Amanda Kassar, Molly McQueen, and Amanda Kloots.